A Potter's Workbook

A Potter's Workbook

Clary Illian

Photographs by

Charles Metzger

University of Iowa Press

Iowa City

University of Iowa Press, Iowa City 52242

Copyright © 1999 by the University of Iowa Press

All rights reserved

Printed in the United States of America

http://www.uiowa.edu/~uipress

Printed on acid-free paper

All photos are by Charles Metzger except the following: page 93, right, Tom Mills; page 94, top, Peter Lee; pages 20 and 97, top left, Hubert Gentry; and page 103, bottom, Mary Rezney.

Library of Congress Cataloging-in-Publication Data

Illian, Clary, 1940–

    A potter's workbook / by Clary Illian; photographs by Charles Metzger.

        p.   cm.

    Includes bibliographical references.

    ISBN 0-87745-671-2 (paper)

        1. Pottery—Design.   2. Pottery—Technique.

I. Metzger, Charles.   II. Title.

NK4225.I45   1999

738.1—dc21   98-52161

03   P   5

A real tradition is not the relic of a past that is irretrievably gone; it is a living force that animates and informs the present. . . . Far from implying the repetition of what has been, tradition presupposes the reality of what endures. It appears as an heirloom, a heritage that one receives on condition of making it bear fruit before passing it on to one's descendants.

IGOR STRAVINSKY, POETICS OF MUSIC IN
THE FORM OF SIX LESSONS

Any great craft tends at last toward a condition of philosophy.

ROBERTSON DAVIES, WORLD OF WONDERS

Contents

Acknowledgments

I thought asking Charles Metzger to do the photos for this book would be a good idea. It turned out to be an inspired idea. Charles is a professional photographer whose passion has shifted to making pots. He not only knew how to photograph the examples but why we were photographing them. In addition, he processed all the images digitally, an art form in itself. I cannot thank him enough for his expertise, generosity, and belief in the project.

The photographs are of green pots made in workshop situations. I felt that black-and-white photographs taken of pots in an unfinished state would keep the emphasis on basic form without introducing the personality of individual makers. Thanks to my assistants and students at Penland, the Jill Hinkley Studio in Washington, D.C., and the Chester Springs Studio in Pennsylvania who so cheerfully gave permission to use photographs of their pots without attribution. Thanks also to the leadership of these institutions for their unhesitating support. The depicted pots are not meant to be standards of perfection or a catalog of possibilities. They are designed to illustrate the points made in the text.

My writer friend Linda Robinson Walker was my first reader and editor. Her wonderfully partisan but thorough marking of the manuscript enabled me to send it out into the world with confidence. Mary Barringer, Gerry Williams, Jack Troy, and Val Cushing all gave me helpful readings.

Finally, just to prove that the making of pots is a charmed activity, some faithful customers revealed to me at exactly the perfect time that they made books. Thanks to Holly Carver and Karen Copp of the University of Iowa Press for making the publishing of *A Potter's Workbook* a painless, even joyous, experience.

A Potter's Workbook

Truth to Process

A Potter's Workbook is a utilitarian pottery workshop in a book. It is designed to help students who are learning to throw pots, potters who know how to throw but feel the need for greater understanding, and skilled craftspeople who enjoy thinking about the objects they love. My aim is to provide a way to see, to make, and to think about the forms of wheel-thrown vessels. Workbooks have exercises, and this book is no exception. The assigned exercises that begin each chapter are designed not only to explain the mechanics of throwing and finishing pots but also to introduce a corollary theoretical framework—a sort of textbook for the hand.

Bernard Leach published *A Potter's Book* in 1940. It has served as a source of information and inspiration for generations of participants in the modern studio pottery movement. The title of this book, *A Potter's Workbook*, pays tribute to Leach's book and in particular to the notion of truth to process evident in his own work and in the work he revered. Leach, an Englishman, studied ceramics in China and Japan in the early years of the twentieth century. In 1920 he returned to England to set up a pottery in St. Ives, Cornwall. His lifetime mission was to train potters and to introduce to the West the aesthetic standards he perceived in the great pottery of the East.

As an apprentice at the Leach Pottery in 1964 and 1965, I helped produce a line of standard ware shapes. I remember vividly the moment when I realized that I was not learning shapes but processes, and that the way a thing is made and its appearance are one and the same.

Leach said, "The method by which a pot is formed determines its general character, whether hand-modeled or built up out of coils or slices, or freely thrown on the wheel . . . each process conditions the interpretation of the original idea, and each has limited range of right usage, from the easy-flowing application of which follows the sense of satisfaction and adequacy of technique. . . . The beauty of each method lies in using that method honestly, for what it is worth, not in imitating other quite different processes."[1]

Although most of what I have to say is an appendix to the idea of truth to process, it does not mean that I narrow the definition of quality to pots produced only in this way. I can well imagine wheel-thrown utilitarian forms that disguise, deny, or defy truth to process and yet are wonderful. This book is limited to a discussion of pots made simply on the wheel and the principles of form arising from that method. I believe that all beginning throwers need to start by mastering truth to process.

There are many ways to achieve the same ends, and so my descriptions of the making processes will dwell more on the purpose of the motions than on precise hand positions. "Whatever works" is always the most honest instruction. The emphasis is not on how to do but why to do. This book will explore sound, lively, and economically produced pottery forms that combine an invitation to mindful appreciation with ease of use.

Studying form and structure leads inevitably to making generalizations and dividing the infinite variety of pots into classes. It is a bit like the naming of plants and animals—a convenient method of making sense out of endless manifestations. However, like plants and animals, pots don't come with names and value judgments attached. They occupy the physical world in many permutations for many purposes. I offer the descriptions, generalizations, and classifications not as absolute truths but as starting points for learning. Not for a minute do I think that words are the same as physical things or that the particular words I have chosen are the only words that can point the way.

The isolated beginning potter may want to use this book as an instruction manual following the assignments in order and using the discussion as checkpoints. Students and teachers who are in community might prefer to dip into the book at will to stimulate projects and debate. Experienced potters might enjoy revisiting the descriptions of generic shapes as a way to jump-start their creative engines. The chapters on seeing, learning, developing style, and finding a place in society can be taken separately as doses of personal biography, clarifying context, building morale, or infuriating rhetoric.

I read many books and articles to prepare to write this book and realized with chagrin that most of the ideas I had thought unique to me were already beautifully described by others. It seems that our experience leads us to similar conclusions, each of us reinventing the meaning of wheel-thrown forms all over again. And so this book is a compendium of ideas, some my own, some held communally, and some so illuminating that they are gratefully acknowledged by quotes and endnotes.

Wondrous

It is a wondrous thing that long after it has ceased to be necessary, people still want to make pots on the potter's wheel. And luckily for the people who want to make them, there are still people who want to use them. In fact, the number of makers and users grows and grows. What is the attraction?

Perhaps for the makers it is the clay that ensnares. It has so many associations with childhood memories of messing around in the mud; the lovely squish, the pies and pellets, the "let's pretend" scenarios of use. In adulthood clay still feels just as luscious and still amazes just as much in its response to our every touch. Although it seems alive because it can move, it does so only because we pinch and twist and roll it with the die of our hands.

Many see the magic of throwing a pot and decide then and there they must possess it, they must learn it. Perhaps it has the lure of any activity that looks hard but doable, like skiing or dancing or juggling. At this point the pottery product is secondary to the imagined kinesthetic pleasure of successfully performing the movements.

I was so besotted by learning to throw that I talked about it in my sleep, and to this day it is the reason for my involvement with clay. When I sit down at the wheel, I anticipate pleasure mixed with not a little anxiety. Will I be able to make a good pot? Will I be able to make a pot at all? Success is never certain.

Some people fall in love with the pots rather than the process. They are so eager to make them that they stay plugged in through the frustrating first steps of learning to throw. They have been seduced by fired clay toasted to the colors of autumn, the semiprecious stone of glazes, and the curve of a bowl in the hands. The imaginative projection centers on the fantasy of making their own dishes.

Whatever the point of entry, in time students become aware of the pots around them in the studio, and these pots become models. Immediate influences are often transparent to a student in the midst of the thrill of acquiring new skills, but in order to mature in the craft it is important to think through how we learn about pottery form. It would be nice to believe that pottery shapes just well up from within. Perhaps they would if we lived in cultural isolation. Perhaps then we would take our ideas from nature: spheres from the moon, slender columns from the trunks of trees, shallow bowls from meadow ponds, and animated profiles from the human body. But we do not live in isolation, and once we have seen pots we lose innocence and begin to learn their morphology much as we begin to learn a language. You might say we have a disposition to make shapes, but the manifestations are expressed in the particular visual language we happen to learn.

The language that surrounds us can be an asset or a liability. Think, for example, of learning to make pots in a Japanese pottery village during the Edo period between 1615 and 1868. Generation after generation of farmer/potters explored and refined the same shapes using local materials and coaxing the best firings from their kilns. Bernard Leach used to marvel at the quality of folk pots from the past. It seemed to him that folk potters could hardly make a bad pot.

Learning from the pots of unskilled or unsophisticated students is less advantageous. Students make predictable shapes when they are still struggling with the basics and cannot place the clay where they want it (preferably well up into the walls of the pot rather than hovering somewhere down around its ankles). They have not been exposed to the principles of good form, nor do they have minds stocked with images of sound, handcrafted pots.

Indeed, we all have minds stocked almost exclusively with images of machine-made objects. These objects are not bad in themselves, but machines utilize different processes and produce forms designed to rigid specifications and subject to complete regulation during fabrication. The profiles and surfaces lack the nuance and diversity that are a natural outcome of the risk-taking nature of making pots on the wheel.

In the book *The Nature and Art of Workmanship* David Pye constructs a continuum of manufactured objects, placing those made by machines in "the workmanship of certainty" and those made by hand in "the workmanship of risk." Although the wheel is described as a self-regulating tool with each revolution of the clay through the fingers acting as a guide for the next, pottery is clearly made by the workmanship of risk.[1] The outcome is dependent upon the judgment and skill of the thrower from moment to moment. The potter should not confuse perfection of skill with mechanical perfection of surface and silhouette.

The following chapters will introduce the principles of good form and good forming. The two are intertwined. Once you are aware of them, you have a better chance of making good pots even from the beginning while you are still learning to move the clay. As you get better you can learn to manipulate the principles and ultimately to stretch them. It is only in understanding the anatomy of good form that you can create afresh.

This workbook focuses on utilitarian pottery form created on the potter's wheel. Different methods of working with clay and different intentions open up other possibilities, but working on the wheel imposes specific limitations. Shapes are circumscribed because of the nature of clay, gravity, centrifugal force, and the potter's hands. Just as the skeleton of an animal must be organized according to certain principles in order to support and contain the body and allow for movement, so too are pots limited to a certain underlying geometry. This has confused modern practitioners mightily as they try to reconcile the demand for innovation of contemporary art with the inevitably familiar results of shapes made on the wheel. Although wheel-thrown pots are endless in their variations, they resolve into types of shapes linked by silhouette and structure.

Morphological charts of pottery types are not lively and may appear to have nothing to offer a student newly hooked on throwing pots, but they are a distillation of thousands of years of pottery history, and this history is of the utmost importance. Learning the categories of shapes made both in the past and by present-day folk potters is just as important to the potter as the study of human anatomy is to the figurative artist or the study of grammar to the aspiring writer. They teach structure. Studying examples of pots in books, museums, and, best of all, in the homes of collectors teaches options and standards. To refuse to learn ceramic history for fear of inhibiting creativity or personal expression is foolish. Images from the past are the potter's grammar and vocabulary.

Pots are improvisations upon given themes and should be celebrated as such. In *The Book of Laughter and Forgetting* Czech writer Milan Kundera explains the richness of this kind of specialized creativity with these words: "Let me try to explain it by means of an analogy. The symphony is a musical epic. We might compare it to a journey through the boundless reaches of the external world, on and on, farther and farther. Variations also constitute a journey, but not through the external world. You recall Pascal's pensée about how man lives between the abyss of the infinitely large and the infinitely small. The journey of the variation form leads to that second infinity, the infinity of internal variety concealed in all things . . . The variation form is the form of maximum concentration. It enables the composer to limit himself to the matter at hand, to go straight to the heart of it . . . The journey to the second infinity is no less adventurous than the journey of the epic, and closely parallels the physicist's descent into the wondrous innards of the atom." [2]

What is the heart of the matter in pottery making? To call into being an object and to ask the object to have qualities that evoke in the viewer a sense of rightness, beauty, or vitality is to tinker with the divine. Making pots offers a constant challenge to search for the mysterious underpinnings of the physical world itself. It is no wonder that "structure, most easily understood when presented visually, has much of the character of a universal metaphor." [3]

The Space Within

The assignment is to make a cylinder, somewhat taller than it is wide, that suggests the greatest possible internal empty space for the given amount of clay. It is the suggestion of space we are concerned with, not the measurable space. The goal is to create an internal space whose lively presence speaks for itself. Slight modulations of the silhouette are permissible, as are variations in treatment of the bottom and top edges of the wall of the pot. Do not think of this as a completed pot, and do avoid bulky rim shapes. If you are doing this assignment in a group, you should all use the same amount of clay.

Each time I've done this exercise with students at the beginning of a workshop the result has been edifying but unpredictable. As you settle down to look at the cylinders, acknowledge your tastes and clear your mind of likes and dislikes. Taste is built upon personal history and emotional associations, and it is important to move on to more objective observation. When the discussion is over, you will not have a simple equation that says a particular shape equals the suggestion of maximum internal space but, instead, a whole list of the visual components of a cylinder and how they interact to speak of the space within.

Putting visual perceptions into words is tricky. I have often criticized a weakness in one of the components of a pot only to realize that it would not be a weakness if another component were changed. The underlying perception is that something is not quite right, but the angle of verbal attack may contain only a partial truth if it does not discuss the reciprocal actions of all the parts. For the purposes of this book I have posited simple causal relationships that break the act of seeing into manageable chunks of instruction. Your understanding depends upon my choice of salient verbal descriptions and appropriate visual examples and your willingness to accept them as tools rather than rules.

The most obvious visual component of a cylinder is the shape. By shape I mean the profile of the object: its silhouette through a complete rotation in space. The directive that the cylinder be taller than it is wide has already partially determined the aspect of its shape called proportion, that is, the relationship of height to width. It would be difficult to compare the internal volumes of shapes with radically different proportions. Figures 1–6 depict a typical set of shapes made for this assignment.

7

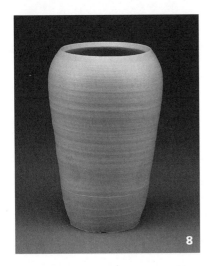

8

One might anticipate that convex shapes would best succeed at appearing to be filled with air. Outwardly bulging walls would seem to guarantee an impression of maximum internal volume, but equating convexity with capacity turns out to be too simple. A swelling profile can have many different dynamics. If the swelling occurs low in the shape, the sagging volume seems affected by gravity, and some of the energy drops into the surface below the pot rather than suggesting a fullness throughout (figure 7). If the swelling rides high in the shape, the rising energy may also detract from a sense of maximum containment (figure 8). Or, perhaps, the convex curve is flattened, creating a constricting corset (figure 9). If it is a uniform, uninflected curve, its static quality may prevent the impression of lively space. Curiously, it is often a slightly concave form that best fulfills the volumetric goal. Concave or gently flaring shapes can make a vigorous, breathing column of air (figures 1, 4).

The termination at the top edge also plays a part. If the edge tilts inward, trapping a dark shadow inside the cylinder, it may call attention to the captive air (figure 10); if it tilts out, releasing the eye, it may seem to let the contained air breathe into the space above (figure 11). The bottom termination may likewise influence the impression of capacity. An edge curving inward at the base can hint at bottom heaviness in the wall of the pot, filling up the interior space with clay rather than air (figure 12). A flaring bottom edge could present the column of air in a way that either energizes or chokes the contents (figure 13).

Specifying a cylindrical shape for this assignment has limited the difference between the width of the base and the width of the mouth.

9

10

11

Slight variations between them create the same dynamic as a top edge tipped either inward or outward. A mouth narrower than the base can bind off a taut space like the knot on a well-filled balloon (figure 14), but a wider mouth can pull more air in (figure 15). And so it is evident that hollow shapes have a narrative capability. They tell stories about the ability of the shapes to act upon the air within, to hold it, to release it, to move it, to compress it.

But are these stories, after all, taste—the very pitfall we are trying to avoid? I think instead they are narratives about the space within based on the way we experience and observe the forces of nature acting upon the world of physical objects around us and even upon our own bodies. We interpret these forces personally and individually, but it is a new experience to become aware of them and to share them and to learn that we usually draw the same conclusions.

We have talked about the shapes acting upon the enclosed volumes, but what we are really looking for in this assignment is volumes so enlivened that they seem to act upon the shapes. This impression is conveyed not only by shape, but also by the surface qualities of the walls of the pot. The pressure of fingers or ribs or sponges on the rising clay walls creates a skin on the surface that can vary as widely as the choice of shapes. Is the clay open and grainy or compressed and smooth? Although the throwing process makes the skin of a pot, it often looks as though the contained volume causes the skin quality. A taut, thin skin can be the factor that expresses capacity even more than shape.

Underneath the skin lie the muscles or the record of the movements

14

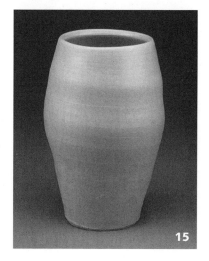

15

12

13

16

17

it took to throw the pot. Another term for this record is gesture: the marks your fingers or tools make as they pull up the walls of the pot, thin them out, and put them into different configurations. Gesture includes the skin tone described before, but also usually gives evidence of the spiraling interaction between the spinning wheel and the rising pulls of throwing. As such, gesture is the notation of the passage of time manifested in the work. Surface texture and gesture are important because they signal human touch and are one of the most obvious ways we identify the work as handmade.

There are innumerable gestural possibilities. The tracks of the force used can vary from the heavily gouged to the whispered; the tracks of the tools used can vary from the knife-edged to the billowy-edged. All of these possibilities can in turn be combined with the tracks of time, that is, the speed of the wheel relative to the speed of the rising pulls of throwing, and can vary from staccato regularity to an unmetered lope (figures 16–19).

The gesture interacts with the shape to tell an increasingly complex story. For example, a convex curve married to a spacious but boldly defined gesture might suggest infinite swelling, but that same curve married to a spacious but rubbery gesture might look like a deflating balloon (figures 20, 21). A very closely spaced, concave gesture with sharp edges might detract from a sense of bursting interior space because of the intense and distracting visual action on the surface (figure 19).

The speed of the gesture traveling up the wall is another part of the interaction with shape and the impression of internal volume, but it

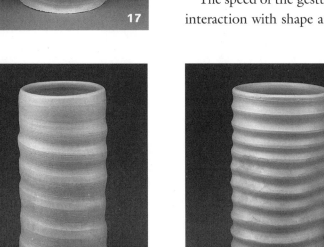

18

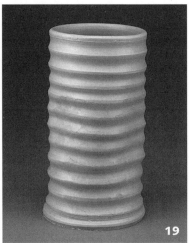

19

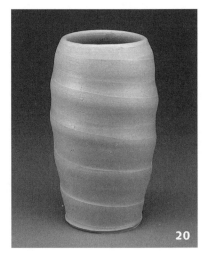

20

is hard for me as an experienced thrower to disentangle specialized knowledge from intuitive response. I do not know what the average viewer makes of these rhythms vis-à-vis volume, and even experienced potters differ in their responses to the spacing of gesture because of the specifics of their training. For a student who knows only a motorized wheel, a staccato gesture might speak of virtuoso throwing and confident volumes (figure 22). But a student who prefers a slower, foot-powered wheel would read a more spacious spiraling as the fast rise of the clay in the hands of a master potter and assume that the clay is well distributed throughout the walls of the pot, creating generous volumes (figure 23).

Profile, terminations, proportion, surface, and gesture all give clues that the clay has been thrown with skill; the walls have been thinned and contoured with no wasted movements, and the clay has retained the impression of tone or elasticity that is one of its definitive characteristics. Efficiency in throwing enlivens the form and the space within.

Why set this assignment first? It is hard to think consciously about volume. The mind keeps slithering away from the subject for fascinating reasons perhaps having to do with the structure of the brain.[1] But if a potter is committed to making pots for use, surely the inside volume is of the utmost importance. It is the very reason for the enveloping clay. And, as we have seen from the discussion of the forms made for the assignment, all of the components of form speak about the space inside, expressing a dialogue with that space.

The task was to make a cylinder. The word "pot" was not used in order to keep the emphasis on the goal of maximum internal space and to avoid the natural desire to make an object that could be judged and found good. Cylinders are often viewed as a sort of warm-up exercise before "real" pots are made, but cylinders are real pots capable of all the complexity of use and aesthetics as other shapes. The second assignment will flesh out this idea, and the third assignment will consolidate it.

Beginnings and Endings

The assignment is rims and bases. Wedge up a few pounds of clay and throw as many different kinds of rims as you can devise. Cut each rim off the cylinder, save it, and then throw another. The term *rim* can apply to a simple, undifferentiated top edge as well as an articulated or protruded terminating shape. Practice variations of bottom edge shapes with separate lemon-size balls of clay, pulling up just enough of the wall to show how it would grow out of the chosen bottom edge treatment.

When you are learning to throw, it may seem that you run out of clay, the wall ends, and that's all there is to it. This is not so. There is more, much more. The wall has an inside surface and an outside surface, and at the top they can meet in many different ways. A decisive treatment, however subtle, tells the viewer that you meant to stop the pot at a given point and in a given way (figures 24–26). At the bottom you also have choices to make about detailing the way the wall of the pot meets the bottom of the pot (figures 27, 28).

I suggest two separate cuts with a wooden knife as a way of finishing the bottom of the pot. The first cut shaves off clay parallel to the wall, and the second cut enters at an angle to the wall at the very base of the pot where it meets the wheel-head. These cuts get rid of the weight at the bottom of a pot, but they have an equally important visual purpose. A clear angled or rounded shape at the bottom edge, part of which makes a shadow under the form, stops the eye and contains its movement within the form. If you look at pots from the past from any culture that used the wheel, you will almost always see a shadow defining the base.

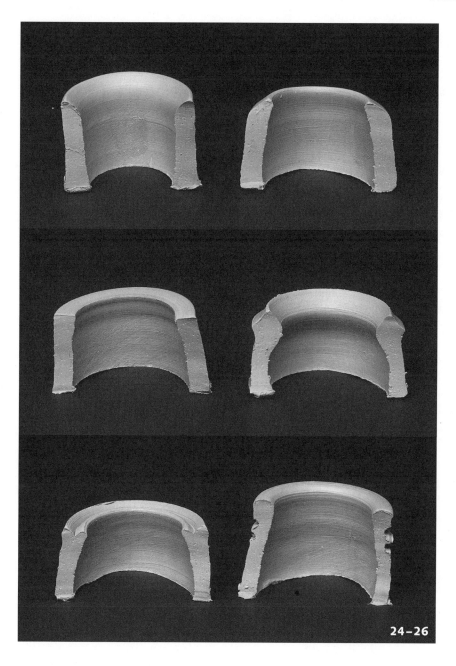

24–26

27, 28

The possibilities of articulated rim and base shapes are endless. Many of them arise from the contours of tools, fingers, and even fingernails. Establish the rim shape early in the throwing process, as early as the second pull, when you still have plenty of clay to work with. Setting the rim is an extension of compressing the top edge after every pull, which you want to do to keep the clay in good health. Pressing down with your thumb on the supported top edge can thicken the wall into a fat, wedge-shaped rim. The gouge of a fingernail or the edge of a rib can complete the articulation (figures 29–31). An additional bonus in setting the rim early is that the thickened shape acts as a reinforcing collar for thinning and shaping the wall below.

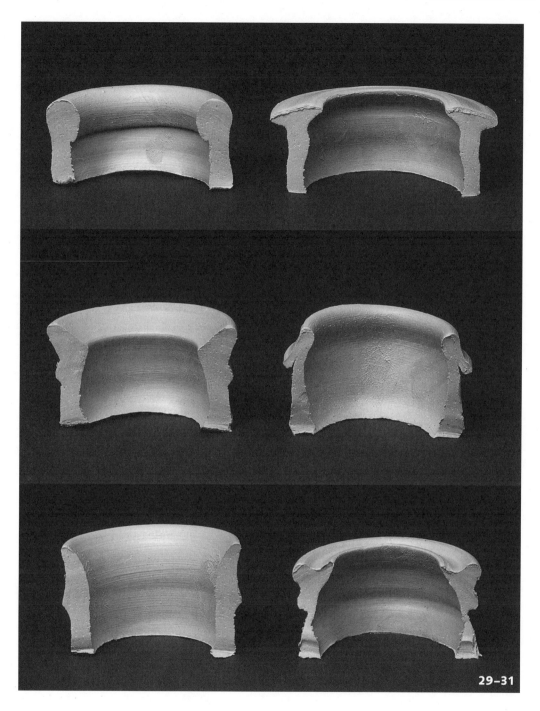

29–31

Base shapes can be simple or complex and are often determined entirely by the shapes of your tools (figures 32–34). Sometimes the rim suggests an echoing response at the base, or perhaps the two might be dissimilar for contrast. Slight thickening or complexity of shape reinforces the bottom of the wall just as it does the top.

The variation in results of this exercise will be greater among people than within the output of any one person. The individual tends to gravitate to similar increments of clay no matter what the shapes. This tendency should be a choice, not an unconscious habit. Remember that just because you are trying to throw thinner and thinner walls does not mean that the top and bottom edges inevitably have to be thin also. Making choices about putting the top, middle, and bottom together is what the next assignment is all about.

32–34

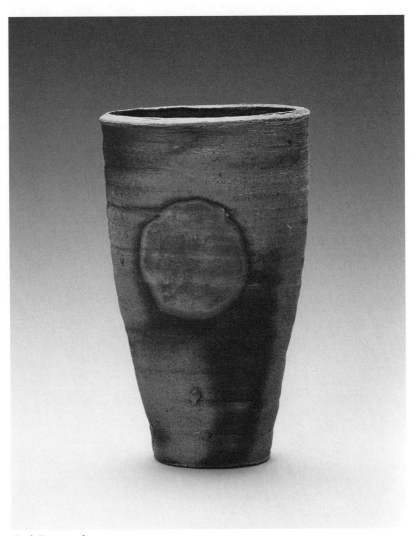

Rob Barnard

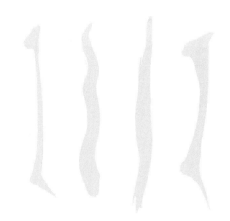

Cylinders as Pots

The third assignment is to throw a cylinder that is not just a throwing exercise but a finished pot—a cylinder with a personality and a story to tell. It can be simple or complex, a bit concave or convex, punctuated with subtle or strong beginnings and endings.

These pots have distinct personalities; they have something to say. The simplest shapes speak of the charm of silhouettes, the animation of the spaces within, and the possibilities of establishing moods. They demonstrate the power of limitations (figures 35–38).

In the chapter "The Space Within" the task of the potter was described as creating volume. Another way to think about making pots is to see the task as one of projecting lines into space. View the walls as lines and look at them as critically as we would look at the lines of a drawing. Do the lines have interest in themselves? Do they have unique characteristics? Are they dynamic? Do they have strong beginnings and endings? Figure 39 shows sketches made of brush and ink lines executed individually, then paired up to generate ideas for cylinders. Where do the ends of the lines send the eye, out into space indefinitely, on an intersecting trajectory, or back into the pot (figures 40, 41)?

Of particular interest to the beginner is the ability to create a shape in which the clay is well distributed throughout the walls of the pot, not only in fact but in terms of the impression it makes. Remember that in the throwing of a vertical form the right hand is dominant. The inside hand acts only as a firm support to counter the strong inward tapering pull of the outside hand. After the cylinder reaches full height, the inside hand can play more of a part in the shaping.

35

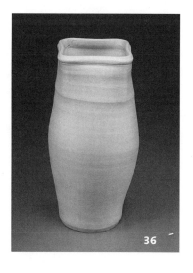

36

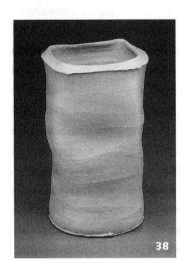

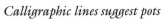
Calligraphic lines suggest pots

To avoid the suggestion of heaviness, be sure that the bottom inch or two describes a plane or concave curve, never a convex curve (figures 42, 43). A rounded bottom suggests that the entire pot is perched upon a foundation that experience tells us cannot possibly bear the weight unless it is very thick. The eye is also robbed of the pleasure of seeing a form that looks like it is standing proud with good support under the volume. Trimming away the extra clay after the pot has stiffened would solve this problem but add an extra process.

Corrected convex base

This assignment stipulates cylinders completed in one session on the wheel. The cause of round-bottomed pots is a failure to open up a wide enough floor with crisp right-angled corners before pulling up the walls (figure 44). During the pulling of the walls you must also be careful not to unconsciously push out with your inside hand at the bottom, altering the upward flow of the clay. At the end of the throwing process, trim off the slight skirt of extra clay at the bottom with a wooden knife and correct the transition between the trimmed area and the thrown area, bringing the whole profile into true vertical.

More complicated shapes teach an additional lesson. If you could cut the pots into cross sections, you would notice that there are variations in thickness throughout the walls. These variations contribute a more complex linear quality akin to the brush strokes of Japanese calligraphy with their clear, accented beginnings, middles, and endings and their movements from thick to thin (figure 45).

Variations in thickness within the walls of a pot also contribute sculptural complexity. The walls of each pot are made up of a stack of shapes that have interest in themselves. For example, a cylinder might begin at the base with a beaded shape articulated from the wall by two grooves, move up into space with tapering walls, and be capped with a wedge shape articulated from the wall by a triple groove (figure 46). There are many possible configurations (figures 47, 48).

44

Opened ball of clay with good bottom and inside corner

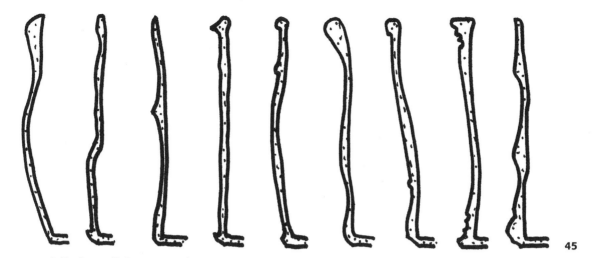

45

Cylinder walls in cross-section

46

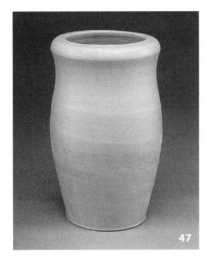

47

48

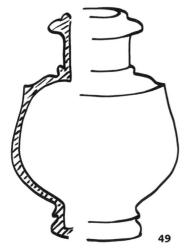

49

Structural variations in wall thickness

And so each pot has two shapes: a shape delineating the volume and a shape within the wall itself. There is no rule that the inside and the outside profiles of the walls must be the same, as is often taught. A more sophisticated sense of form allows for differences between the inside and outside shapes as long as the pot is not bottom-heavy. These differences can offer rich relationships and surprises. Although you cannot see all of the internal wall profile from the outside, you can feel and intuit these variations in thickness in the walls and appreciate the complexity they add.

There is a reason for these variations in thickness beyond mere sculptural delight. Modulations in the walls of the pot function structurally as well as aesthetically. The chapter on beginnings and endings explains that discrete rim and base shapes act as reinforcements while you continue to thin and shape the wall in between. In *Ceramics* Philip Rawson offers this observation: "in the case of a well-structured pot, the appreciator's hand will be able to find and understand the whole sequence of grip patterns the potter used to make it."[1] Why is it necessary to use a whole sequence of grip patterns? Why not simply pull up the walls into uniform thickness using one all-purpose position of your hands and then bend it into the desired silhouette?

The answer is that gravity won't let you. A variety of hand grips and a variety of shapes within the cross section of the walls are what enable the pot to withstand gravity during the forming process. To continue our comparison of parts of pottery form to the human body, we might say that the stacked shapes within the walls are the bones of a pot, and, like bones, they modulate from thick to thin and have complex joints that provide the strength to hold up the body and allow for movement or, in pottery terms, changes of direction (figure 49).

Bill Daley says that structure is "developed through configurations of the wall that conduct gravity and carry weight to rest."[2] As throwers, we might prefer to put the emphasis on moving the clay upward into space and resisting gravity, but the sense is the same.

The pace and vigor of throwing can introduce repeated shape increments within the walls of the pot. One potter's gesture could resemble lenses; another's would appear knobbed at each end like thigh bones; another's might look like teardrops. Gesture with its upward spiral is one of the configurations that tells the story of the wheel and the hands working in time to overcome the force of gravity. It can act alone or as a sort of subtext to the variations of wall thickness caused by the need for reinforcement.

Whatever the shape and structure of a cylinder, whatever the beginning and ending treatments, whatever the gesture and mood, all of the components must be unequivocal. They must manifest what they suggest and avoid what Henry James called the flaw of "weak specification."[3] This demands decision making at every second of the throwing process and well-thought-out ideas that inform those decisions.

And so there is no such thing as "just a cylinder." A cylinder is a shape that can be simple or complex, that can establish a mood and can offer all the metaphorical possibilities of any other shape. The fact that it must be mastered before other shapes can be attempted has given it a low status, but it has value of its own. Its potential for use as well as appearance is endless. A cylinder can be a storage jar, a vase, a mug, or even, as we shall see in the next chapter, a pitcher.

Mark Hewitt

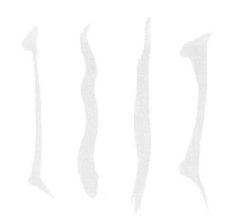

Pitchers

It is time to move on to a specific utilitarian form. The assignment is to make pitchers. Use at least two pounds of clay or more, and keep it simple. Do not make forms that will require turning or trimming, but think in terms of cylindrically derived shapes. Remember that this is an incomplete form, as it will have a handle and a spout added after it is thrown.

The most obvious shapes that could serve well as pitchers are cylinders. Suppose that all the pots made so far had spouts and handles. Nearly all of them would make perfectly adequate pitchers, and some of them would be very exciting to look at and a pleasure to use (figures 50–54).

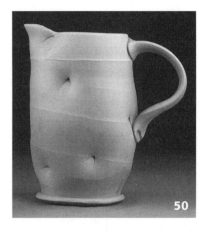

A useful notion for analyzing pitchers comes from Warren MacKenzie. He says pitchers have two parts: a part that contains and a part that delivers the contents (figure 55). Clearly, in the case of simple cylindrical pitchers, there is no distinction between the two parts. But utility is served; there is plenty of room and easy delivery of the liquid. One of the best arguments for this shape is ease of cleaning.

A dynamic variation is a cylinder tapering in toward the top edge. This is a type of pitcher made to perfection in medieval England and copied by Bernard Leach in his own work and in the standard ware made by workers at his pottery. It has the elegance of a woman in long, flowing skirts. Many subtle and satisfying variations can be improvised upon it: the profile can stand ramrod straight or curve sinuously. More or less emphasis can hint at the figurative connotations. The containing part is in the voluminous skirts, and the tapering waist and nar-

52

row shoulder deliver the liquid in a controlled manner. Again, the two parts and two functions merge (figure 56).

The opposite shape—a cylinder tapering to the base—is almost never seen in pitchers of any size. In such a shape the containing part is too high for both physical and psychological comfort, and the delivery part with its flared opening would deliver the contents in an uncontrollable gush. However, small pitchers, which would tend to be seen from above while in use and lightweight even when filled, can be made of this inverted shape without fear of accident (figures 57, 58).

53

54

55

Two parts of a pitcher

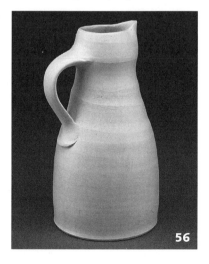

56

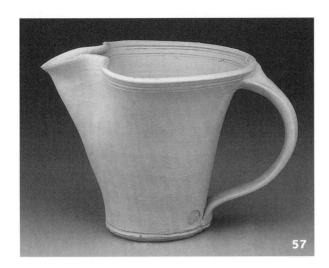

57

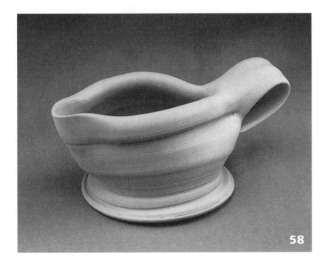

58

When pitcher shapes go wrong, the reason can often be found in a mismatch between the containment and delivery parts. For example, an almost vestigial delivery section perched upon a generous containment section means trouble. There is not enough space for the transition from containing to pouring; the unrestricted liquid must suddenly narrow down to the width of the spout. The moment the user tips the pot, the contents are at the edge (figure 59).

Many pitcher shapes grow more directly out of the idea of separate containing and delivering functions (figures 60–63). You can see that the two functions begin to have two shape units calling for a clear concept about their relationship. Are they distinct with a crisply de-

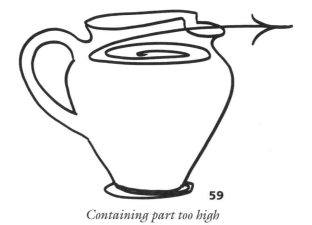

59

Containing part too high

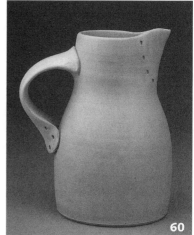

60

61

fined change in the contour, or are they joined by a curve of unfaltering momentum?

Causing particular problems are pitchers whose delivery portions offer sufficient room for efficient pouring but are so narrow that you cannot get your hand inside for cleaning. These shapes are vexing because they are among the most seductive with their elegant and complex lines and, therefore, call for difficult decisions in the balance between aesthetics and utility (figures 64, 65).

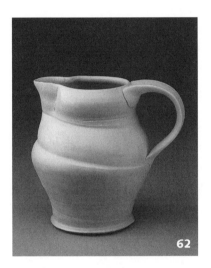

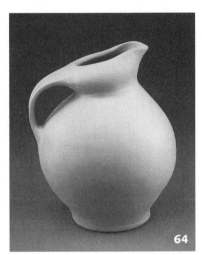

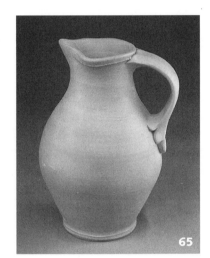

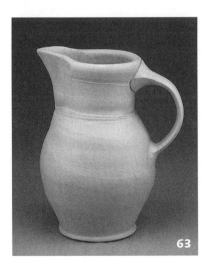

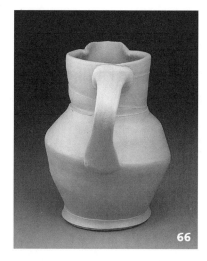

66

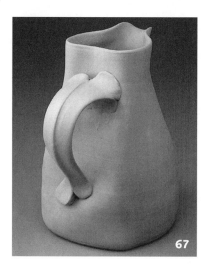

67

The figurative analogy that comes so readily to mind when thinking about pots also applies to the next part of the assignment: handles and their placement. Handles can be thought of as arms, and like arms they need to be thicker at the place where they join on to the body. This gives not only physical but psychological strength at the point stressed most by lifting.

Handles can have almost any shape in cross section. They can be round, strap-shaped, or triangular and any variation in between. A single handle can even change its cross-sectional shape, flowing, for example, from round to half-round and then flattening to a strap at the attaching end. Although traditionally handles often taper from top to bottom, they can flare out at the end or shrink in the middle of the arc with equal thickness at top and bottom ends. They can be further complicated by stroking marks, ridges, or decorative texturing. The possibilities are endless (figures 66, 67).

Choosing a handle requires seeking direction from the pitcher itself. Qualities of throwing, such as gesture and thickness of walls, especially at the mouth of the pitcher, will suggest echoing qualities in the choice of handle. A distinct rim shape might offer the same solution repeated in the handle (figures 68, 69). It might work well to choose a handle that, rather than reiterating some aspect of the pot, is in complete contrast to it. There is no one correct handle for any given pot but several options, each one of which establishes a different set of relationships and a different mood.

Potters often have rigid rules about the shapes and placement of handles that they say feel and work most successfully. But the fact that

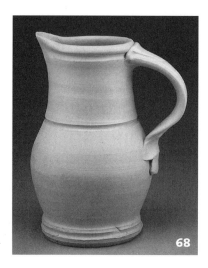

68

69

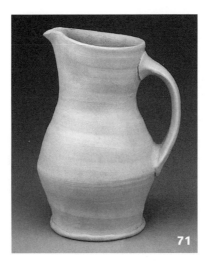

70

71

the utilitarian defense is offered for quite a variety of solutions indicates that this is a subjective matter. Perhaps the most that can be said of handles is that they should not sabotage use by being uncomfortable to grasp, and they should not be placed so that the pot is awkward to lift and pour.

If you remember the armlike quality of a handle, you will be in no doubt where to attach it. The handle begins at the point corresponding to a shoulder and ends on the part suggesting a hip. The arm spans an arc between shoulder and hip in just the same way it does on our bodies (figures 70, 71). And so, too, does the handle span the containing and delivering parts of the form.

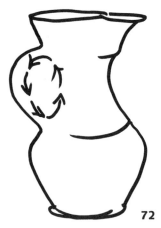

72

Reading the negative space

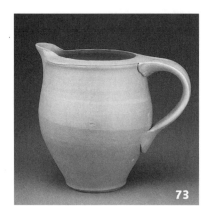

73

Another help in deciding on handle placement is the analysis of negative space. Often a concave portion of the silhouette sets up an elliptical movement of the eye and begs for completion in the curve of a handle (figure 72). It is harder to decide what to do with a form made up only of convex curves. One solution might be to begin the handle high on the form, continuing the plane of the rim (figure 73). This type of shape also causes difficulty in handle placement because of the abrupt transition between the containing and delivery functions, so that the handle has to make up for lack of vertical space by springing out horizontally (figure 74). Pitchers that resemble the Kool-Aid logo with its convex curves, blocky proportions, and horizontal format make for hard leverage at any size beyond the very small (figure 75).

The principle behind the angle of attachment is that the lines of movement set up by the handle should penetrate into the pot, directing the eye into the volume to be lifted (figure 76).[1] This explains why handles attaching parallel to the form are not satisfying. The eye makes two trips, one around the outline of the pitcher and another around the outline of the handle. The two parts are merely adjacent and do not involve one another (figure 77). Convex curves can be managed by imagining the angle of attachment at a right angle to the wall of the pot (figures 78, 79).

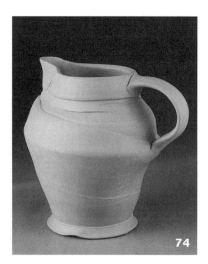

74

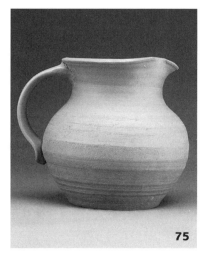

75

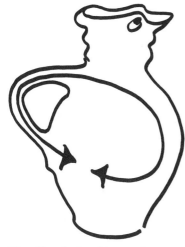

Handle relationship to volume

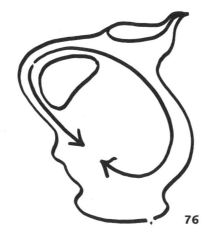

76

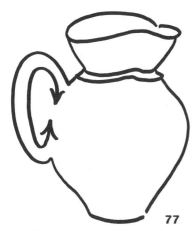

77

Inadequate handle attachment

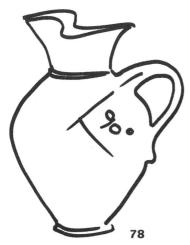

78

*Handle relationship to convex
curve*

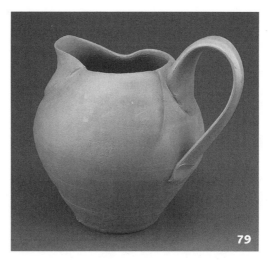

79

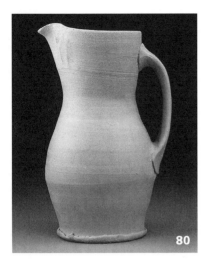

80

Should the handle in profile have a half-round curve, an angled bend, a dropping arc, or a rising arc? Look to the shape for directions. There are lines of movement you can continue or repeat and choices that will emphasize or change the balance of the form (figures 80–84).

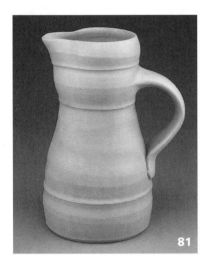

81

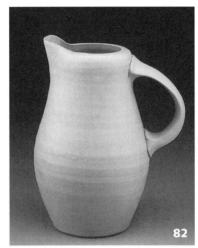

82

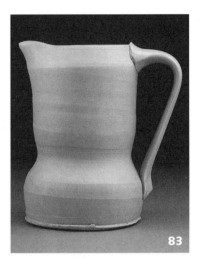

83

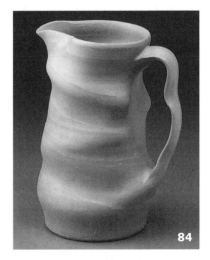

84

A strong horizontal line just below the rim of a pitcher begins a movement of the eye that can logically be continued by the handle. This continuing line must be carried by the curve of the handle and, in the case of handles with sharp outside edges, by those leading visual edges (figure 85). A handle with a rectangular cross section and blunt sides rarely works because the blocky edge stops the eye and does not relate to any other increment of thickness on the pot (figure 86). The outermost edges of a handle offer an opportunity to echo the shape and dimension of the top edge or the articulating edge of a turned-down cuff so the disparate parts appear to be made of the same stuff.

85

Continued horizontal movement in handle

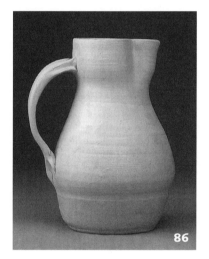

86

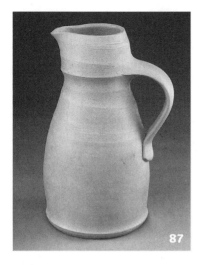

87

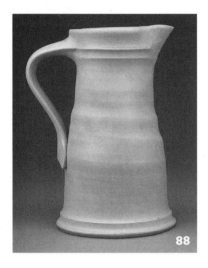

88

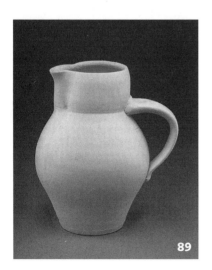

89

A rim with a thickening or a fold below the top edge is a common way to introduce horizontal movement across the form and to strengthen the wall where the handle is attached. It is an excellent example of sculptural form within the wall of the pot itself. The difference between the slight bulge on the outside and the flat wall on the inside delights the eye and makes a smooth pathway for the liquid. I call this a cuffed rim. It can have many permutations (figures 87, 88).

Although I have called your attention to elements in the body of the pitcher that guide the shape and placement of handles, remember there are no hard and fast rules. Some pitcher shapes set up more than one logical place for their handles. Figure 89 shows a double-curved pitcher that could have been spanned by a handle starting in the middle of the top bulge and ending in the middle of the bottom bulge. Instead the handle is placed to continue the horizontal line dividing the two curved sections but softly tucked into that fold in such a way as to echo the rolling volumes of the rest of the pot. Handle and pot are similar in substance and feeling.

Decisions about a handle's appropriate size, shape, and placement are usually made at eye level, but remember the view from the top. Looking down into the pitcher is the view you have while using it, and that view should have the same complexity of relationship as the side view. In most cases the handle should widen where it flows out of the pot, just as it is desirable that it thicken at the point of attachment when viewed from the side (figures 90a, 90b). Without this flow the transition between handle and container looks like a two-by-four butted into a wall (figure 91). The shape and dimensions of a single handle can vary from top to bottom when viewed head-on, just as they can vary when viewed in profile.

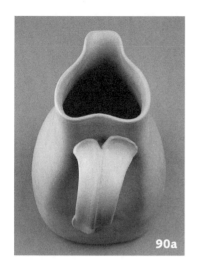

The beginnings and endings of handles must be dealt with by employing the same clarity of intention you used on the beginnings and endings of the pot itself. Does the handle simply flow out of the pot seamlessly, or does it abut to the pot with a clear, articulated shape? The same decision must be made at the bottom attachment. Review all of the illustrations with these points in mind. All details add sculptural complexity and define style.

All the discussion about pitchers to this point is also applicable to the making of mugs. One of the last shapes that student potters master is the mug. This might seem surprising since a mug is such a small and circumscribed object. In the pitcher are all the components of a good mug, for example, the importance of clearly articulated beginnings and endings. Because the mug is small, there is a tendency to think of it as footless and headless, changing it from a complete visual thought into a mere phrase. The triple challenges of volume, delivery, and ease of cleaning still apply. Mug handles have all the potential for richness and relatedness as they have in their larger cousins. The only new element is the drinking rim, which must be comfortable and not cause dribble. Pitchers are a wonderful source of ideas for the shapes of mugs (figures 92–97).

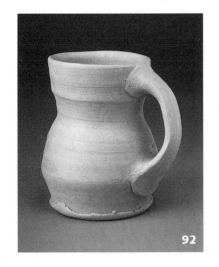

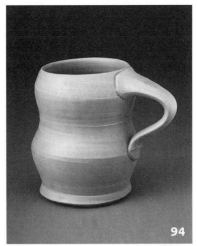

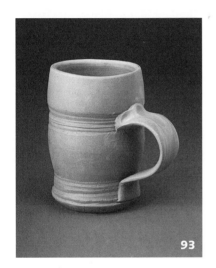

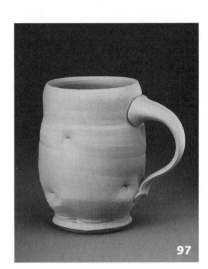

98

99

The definitive element in a pitcher is the spout. Let's begin with the view from the top and look again at the shape and size of the handle where it attaches to the pot. An obvious relationship is the one between the width of the handle and the width of the spout. Making them equal creates movement across the diameter of the opening (figure 98). But, once again, this is not a rule, and it is easy to imagine a spout width relating to something else in the form.

The shape of the spout, viewed from the top, is limited only by functional success. Too narrow a shape chokes the liquid and slows pouring. A broad, semicircular shape can make the liquid fan back and forth across the edge with disastrous results (figures 99, 100). Whatever the shape, the purpose is to provide a channel to guide the liquid to the pouring edge.

The side view of a spout can vary widely, setting up subsidiary configurations with distinct edges or flowing in an unbroken curve from the wall of the pitcher (figure 101). The only question is, once again, will it pour?

Often students are taught that there must be two grooves along the sides of the throat of the spout or it will not pour well. This is not true and can be a trap unless the lines are executed with certainty and relate to all of the parts of the form. Any mark made on the clay must have all the quality of a good drawing mark. It must have interest in itself (figures 102, 103).

100

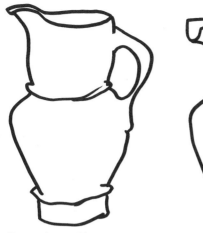

101

Spouts in profile

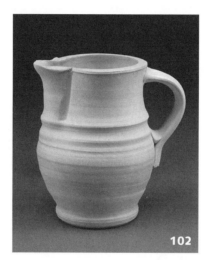

102

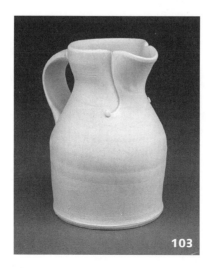

103

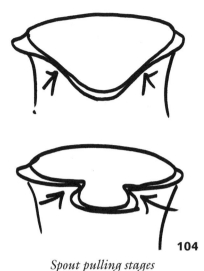

Spout pulling stages

104

But it is true that the area where the spout grows out of the rim and walls must be attended to. After the spout is stretched into a shape, it is necessary to reaffirm the original shape out of which it grows and to decide what happens where the spout and the encircling rim meet (figure 104). The mouth of the pot does not always have to be round. There are other possibilities (figures 105–110). Note also the shapes of the spouts.

Spouts can be applied instead of pulled for an almost endless array of graceful, forceful, or wacky appendages (figures 111, 112). The nose might lead the body; spouts, once invented, suggest body shapes rather than the other way around. These pitchers illustrate a very important component of form, not mentioned thus far. As the eye travels down the slope of the spout across the body of the pitcher it comes to the falling curve of the handle, a strong diagonal movement. Gesture can reinforce or introduce diagonal movement, as can sensitive placement of the secondary pieces of form: handles, spouts, lugs, knobs, and decorative doodads.

In this age of bottled drinks, plastic milk jugs, and coffee-making machines, a pitcher—the intermediary for the delivery of liquids—might seem obsolete. It has become a shape for hospitality or a way to make everyday serving acts special. A pitcher is a family pot, a party pot. It can be a squat and humble perfection in constant use or an imposing and elegant presentation for a public occasion. Because of the armlike handle, the mouthlike spout, and the upright and curvaceous shape, it is a form that easily takes on the animation of the animal kingdom and thereby enchants us with personality.

105

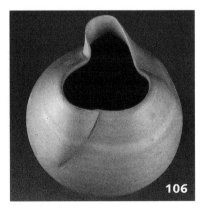

106

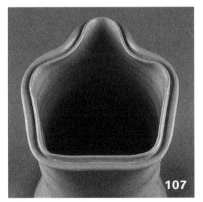

107

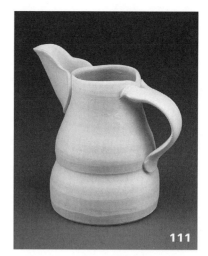

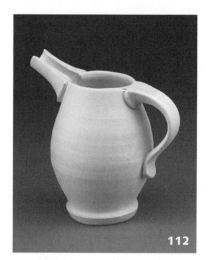

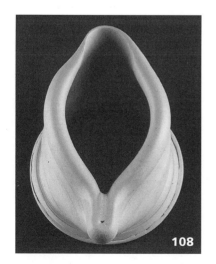

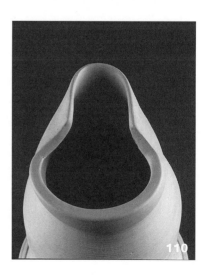

Jeff Oestriech

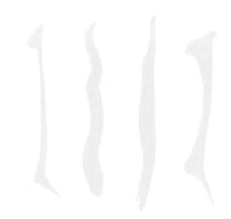

Bowls

Bowls require a complete change of tactics, so clear your mind before tackling them. The assignment is to make bowls with simple open curves. Leave about an inch of unformed clay at the bottom of the bowls to allow for choices of height, width, and shape of turned feet. Use about four pounds of clay.

Centrifugal force causes the walls of a pot to flare, so bowls are a very natural product of the throwing process. The continuously curving inner profile seems simple, and some teachers prefer to start students out on bowls. However, though simple, bowls are not easy. It is hard to make a continuous, uninterrupted curve. Australian potter Gwyn Hanssen Pigott told me, "My teacher, Ivan McMeekin, taught me that from the beginning a bowl must feel like a bowl—not like a cylinder or straight-sided open shape that will later be curved. 'It opens and grows,' he said, 'from bud to full-blown.'"

The "what" of a pot is always inseparable from the "how" of its making, but bowls especially seem to exemplify this link. Because the clay is cantilevered out from a narrow base, gravity, always the potter's enemy, becomes an even greater factor, and bowls cannot be fussed over. They must be made with economy of movement and time. Even more than in the throwing of cylinders, each movement can sabotage the next.

When making bowls the centered mass of clay should have a different shape from the centered mass for a cylinder. Begin with a centered mass shaped like a bulb on a stem and maintain the stem as you open up (figure 113). This shape is similar to the centered portion at the top of a cone of clay when the technique of throwing off the hump is used.

113

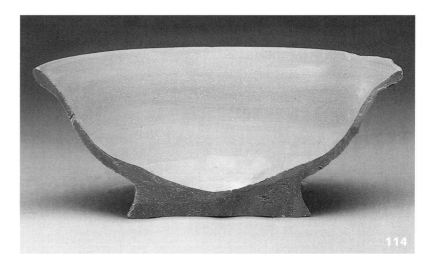

It takes awhile to develop the judgment to determine what proportion of the clay belongs in the stem part and what proportion in the base, but it is worth the struggle, because once you set up the centered mass correctly, the rest comes more easily.

"From the beginning a bowl must feel like a bowl." This means that the lowest point must be in the center, and the curve must rise, however slightly, from that center point. The most difficult task for a beginner is erasing traces of bottoms and sides as separate parts of the form. Bottom/side thinking shows up as a hesitation in the curve or, even worse, as the dreaded beginner's hump (figure 114).

A beginner's hump often shows up as a kink or a small, convex-shaped bulge in the inner profile located at the point where the stem-like platform of clay changes to a cantilevered curve. This is an interruption in the curve that is the inverse of its overall dynamic. Unconsciously pinching in on the outside wall at the beginning of the curve will surely cause this problem.

It is sometimes as hard to see the beginner's hump as it is to get rid of it. Stop the wheel and sponge the water out of the bottom for a careful look. Cut the pot in half to see what is really there. It is best if you do not establish a pause in the curve, but if you do, simply work over the troublesome area until you have pushed the clay into the trajectory of the curve. If you have thinned the walls of the bowl too much, they will not support your efforts to adjust the clay. The solution is to leave extra clay, especially at the part of the curve where the bowl grows from the stem.

Another way to diagnose a beginner's hump is to observe that it creates a pit in the bottom. It helps some people to see the problem when it is described in this way, but once the pit is there, you have no choice but to start the curve at that depth and compress the hump until it disappears.

If S cracking in the center bottom of the foot ring is a problem after the bowl dries, the solution is compression. Set the bottom of the bowl a little deeper each time you make a thinning pass through the curved shape. This means that the initial level of the bottom will be farther from the wheel-head than is ultimately desired and will be lowered about a quarter of an inch each time you start at the bottom and work through the walls.

The inside of a bowl is akin to the outside of a cylinder: it is the significant part of the form both aesthetically and functionally. It therefore follows that the left or inside hand is dominant, whereas in cylinder throwing the right or outside hand is dominant. The right hand contributes to thinning the wall through the curve, but the left hand establishes the curve of the bowl. The fingers (or ribs) of the left hand push at a right angle to the surface while the outside hand tends to ride parallel to the surface, cradling the curve, supporting it against the thinning pressure of the inside hand.

Two schools of thought offer different methods for flaring the walls of a bowl. One school suggests thinning the walls out in a relatively vertical position and then lowering or flattening the curve. The other suggests thinning the walls along the axis of the ultimate profile of the pot. The advocates of the first school say it results in better compression and, therefore, more strength during manipulation. If you choose this method, you must be extra careful to avoid thinking of the bowl as made up of a bottom and sides, breaking the flow of the curve.

After each thinning pass of the hands, it is important to compress and shape the rim. As the rim gets wider in circumference and thinner, it gets harder and harder to change. Establish the rim shape early when there is plenty of clay, even if the rim has no discrete shape but is just a smooth continuation of the walls. If the rim is to have a separate shape, it is obviously even more important to fashion it early in the process.

Useful interior space is the very definition of a good bowl, and in my experience the final adjustment of the inner curve is an elusive and exacting task. The pot always seems to need yet another pass to plump out the curve and firm up the dynamic flow.

Which curve should you choose? The chapter exercise recommended simple, open curves, but our discussion should touch upon the full range of choices. Cupped curves curl in upon themselves, supported curves flatten out as they ascend, freed curves continue to open, and concave curves bend over backward (figures 115–118). The language used to describe these curves might also describe why you would prefer one over another to use with food. However, the assignment stipulated open bowls, so the supported and freed curves are most appropriate. Curves are not right or wrong in themselves but are part of the dance of the whole piece.

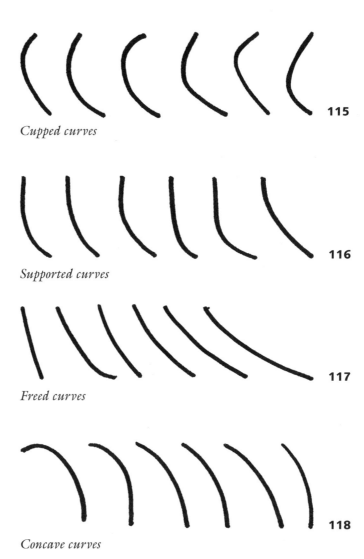

115

Cupped curves

116

Supported curves

117

Freed curves

118

Concave curves

The discussion so far has been about the inner contour. If the inside of a bowl has a satisfying shape and the clay has been well distributed, allowing for extra supporting thickness where the beginner's hump usually occurs, the outside profile will take care of itself. Further attention to the outside is needed only to adjust the gesture or to introduce decorative lines, ridges, or rims. Focusing on the outside profile creates an inside-out look. That is, the exterior is a well-thought-out facade, but the interior feels like the backside and lacks surface compression and a well-defined shape. Because the right hand seems to be the strongest and most "conscious" hand for most people (at least, right-handed people), you might want to try reversing the direction of the wheel so you can shape the interior curve with your right hand to the left of the wheel-head.

The extra thickness supporting the bottom of the curve will be carved away during the turning process (figure 119). When the bowl is dry enough to hold its shape but wet enough that the clay will curl away from the metal cutting tool without sticking, wet the rim to seal it to the wheel-head, turn it upside down, and tap it on center. It is important to find the correct angle of attack with your turning tool (about 45 degrees) and to use muscular tension and bracing to hold the tool steady rather than to transfer force into the bowl. Find the broadest cutting surface possible on the tool. Don't labor over the surface with a pointy, undersized cutting tool but find a generous shaving edge to accomplish the most work with the least effort.

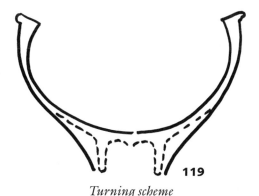

119

Turning scheme

120

121

Feet

Turning a foot is not just a matter of trimming away unwanted clay but an opportunity to make a vital, complementary shape that will present the bowl to best advantage. An adequate stem of unworked clay at the base provides the opportunity to make a choice from a variety of shapes and sizes of foot. Improvise as you work rather than deciding in advance on generic solutions. Choosing the right tools and catching the clay at the perfect degree of wetness allows the metal tool to speak with its own voice, with its own gesture. Treat even the insides of foot rings with respect. When bowls are turned over they should reveal pleasing shapes fashioned with bold strokes of the turning tool. The difference between the thrown surface and the turned surface is subtle but enhancing. Sometimes glazes react differently to the two surfaces, and this can be a wonderful thing. Polishing the surface after you have turned it so that it resembles the thrown surface is usually counterproductive.

While you want to get rid of enough clay to make the bowl feel well balanced and not bottom heavy, don't fret about the inner profile and the outer profile being identical. This is an excellent opportunity to explore the subtle tension and surprise that can occur when the two are different. They are different, after all, as the outside is at least half-formed by the action of the metal tool. Turning actually forms curves by means of a succession of flat planes (figures 120, 121). The result is a cross section capable of the sculptural variation and complexity of vertical pieces.

When you choose a foot shape, you must decide upon the nature of the journey that you want the viewer's eye to take. Do you want an uninterrupted line of movement along the curve already established by the walls of the bowl (figure 122)? Continuing the movement already established by the throwing celebrates the spiral of centrifugal force and is as elegant as a ballet dancer on pointe. Another choice is to continue the line of movement but articulate the foot from the bowl by a defining edge (figure 123). The foot can be made up of one or more planes (figure 124). The tapering angle of the foot can vary up to the point where it appears to be vertical, in which case it makes a very formal presentation (figure 125). If you want a foot to appear to be vertical, you must taper it slightly (figures 126, 127) or, due to an optical illusion, it will look as though it angles back out and changes direction (figure 128).

122

124

123

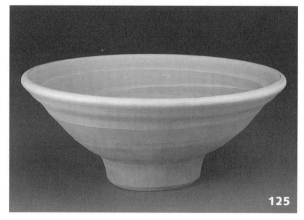

125

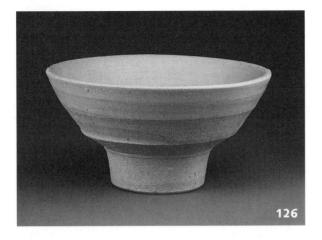

126

127

128

129

Stopping the eye with a foot that changes the direction of the movement is the most commonly seen configuration, a solution probably more automatic than deliberate (figure 129). When making this type of foot, create a higher ring so the eye has time to adjust and revel in the change in direction. Consider whether the form really asks for this type of base. Bowls featuring curves that are true sections of a circle are well complemented by this calm, classical foot (figure 130). The optical illusion of the spreading angle must be compensated for. If the angle of the foot is too oblique, the foot will look as if it is about to collapse upon itself, unable to bear weight. Analyze this foot by finding a center point above the rim of the bowl from which the arc swings and see if the plane of the foot falls along the radii (figure 131). This oblique foot need not be automatically articulated as a plane meeting a curve, but could also be made up of a continual S curve (figure 132).

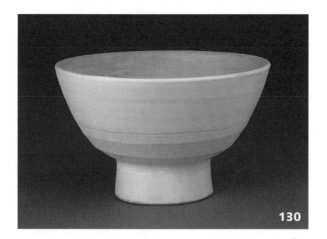

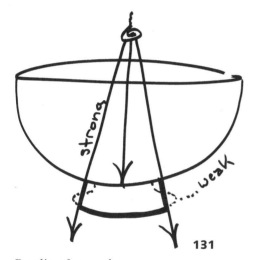

Reading foot angle

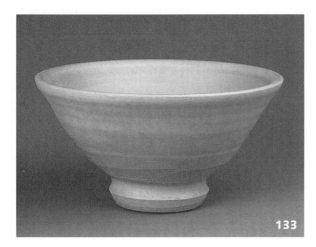

133

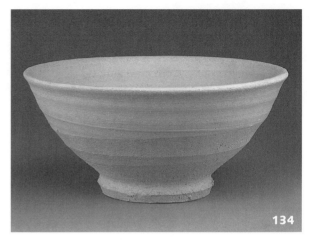

134

The third type of turned foot is a combination of the first two. It is a double-angled foot, or a foot made up of a curve and an angle (figures 133, 134). It takes a lot of experience to learn to combine the proportions and angles of this foot—it often looks unexpectedly different when you turn the bowl right side up. A great trick suggested by Colorado potter Jim Lorio is to place a bat on the foot while it is still on the wheel and upside down, thus enabling a view that more nearly approximates the right-side-up view. One further variation of this foot is a wide, shallow shape that cannot be fully seen from a typical viewing angle but that serves to float the bowl in space, creating a shadow underneath (figure 135).

Generally speaking, it does not make much sense to have a foot thicker in cross section than the walls or rim of the bowl. This thickness cannot be seen and adds unnecessary weight. A small beveled or rolled edge at the bottom of the foot is as important to the bowl as the shadowy undercut that finishes cylindrically derived forms. It stops the movement of the eye and gives clues about the thickness of the clay in cross section. Review all of the illustrations with this in mind.

There are two families of bowls: offering bowls that celebrate freed curves and containing bowls that celebrate cupped curves. Supported curves can fall into either family depending on rim treatments and proportions. Generally speaking, the offering bowl is elegant and courtly while the containing bowl is sturdy and rustic. The proportions of the first are more extreme, moving from very narrow to very wide and releasing the eye to follow the trajectory of the curve into space (figures 136, 137). The second type is more moderate in its movement

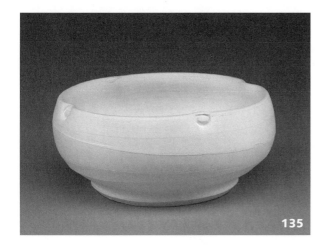

135

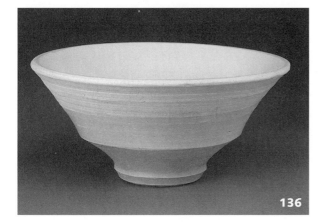

136

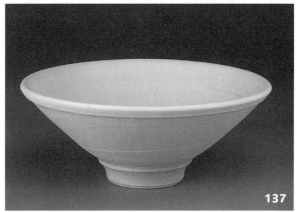

137

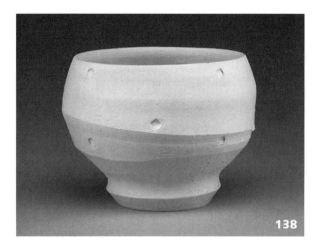

138

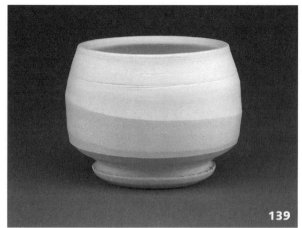

139

from base to rim, trapping the eye inside the shadowy returning walls (figures 138, 139). These categories are artificial, but they provide a way to start thinking about the endless possibilities of bowl shapes. It is certainly true that an elegant courtly bowl could have a rim that stops the eye by curving inward or projecting over the inner profile, creating a shadow. A sturdy country bowl could have a monumentality that makes it fit to serve a king. There is no one perfect foot for a given bowl—different foot choices create different feelings depending upon the potter's aim.

Feet can also be thrown directly on the bowl by attaching a ring of clay to the bottom. This treatment works well for a very tall foot and provides an opportunity to use the same gesture and surface throughout the piece (figure 140). This method emphasizes the "presentation" of the bowl's contents, and the exaggerated size provides a graspable profile beneath the pot.

The assignment specified bowls with feet, but it is also possible to make a bowl with a continuous inner curve and identical continuous outer curve that requires no turning. This is surprisingly hard to do well even on a small scale, but it can be a good exercise for developing judgment at each point in the throwing process. One drawback to this kind of bowl is in function, not the function to the user, but the function a foot has for the potter shepherding the pot through the making, glazing, and firing processes. A stem of clay raises the form to ease access to the bottom of the curve during throwing, and the turned foot acts as a handle while glazing.

Come to think of it, what are feet for? In Eastern cultures, where bowls are held near the mouth to facilitate the use of chopsticks, feet raise the shape for lifting and add a cuff for gripping. In cultures where spoons and forks are used while the bowls are resting on flat surfaces, the foot acts as a stabilizing transition for the round form. It is no accident, therefore, that the inward-sloping foot was brought to perfection in the East, while the kicked-out foot is more typical of European wares. As the modern studio potter movement has matured and borrowed from the great ceramic traditions of the world, the foot that angles in toward the bottom and continues the direction of the curve has become a part of its repertoire.

140

Another option is a bowl with a curved inside and a cylinderlike outer treatment (figure 141). Shallow basin bowls are terrific for soup and pasta, for baking and serving (figure 142). Although it might be possible to complete such a bowl while the pot is still on the wheel, the awkwardness of working under a projecting curve usually requires a second turning process, however simple the outside edge treatment. Basins illustrate, once again, the pleasure of viewing interactions between an outside shape and an inside shape that are not the same. In fact, a basin could simply be a flared cylinder with a flat bottom and discrete sides.

141

142

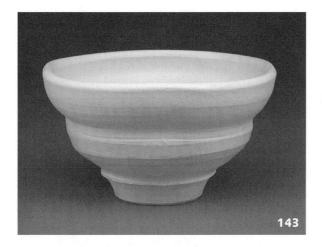

143

145

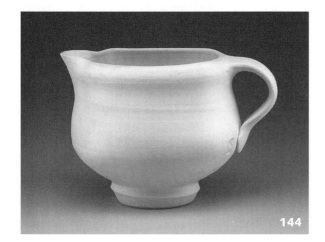

144

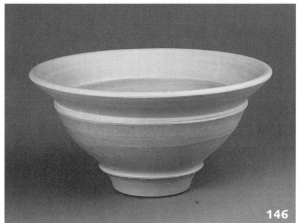

146

147

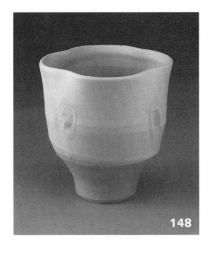

148

150

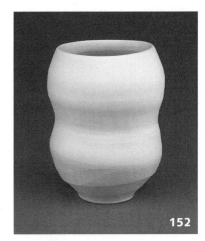

152

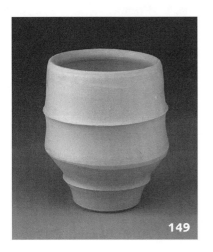

149

151

153

The assignment specified making bowls with simple curves, but bowls can be made up of double or triple curves or curves in combination with planes (figures 143–146). Even the beginner's hump can be turned into an asset (figure 147). Teabowls made for green tea intentionally had a pit in the bottom to trap the sodden leaves.

Teabowls are a special subcategory of bowls. They are really a kind of handleless footed cup. The potter's infatuation with teabowls is another indication of indebtedness to the aesthetic standards of the Far East. While it is possible to educate the public to their use, they are cut loose from their dense cultural moorings and are open to a breadth of improvisation based upon individually defined use and taste (figures 148–153).

Plates

Plates are shallow bowls. All your attention will be focused on the inside while you are making them. Most of your effort will be spent on centering a low, broad mass before you can begin to do the minimal throwing at the outside edge. Take care to avoid beginner's humps and strive for either a clean curve or a shallow basin shape with distinct bottoms and sides. Rim shapes must be very clearly articulated to set them off in the enveloping horizonal format. The back side will be dealt with by turning away excess clay to reveal the shaped edge of either a flat bottom or a raised foot ring (figures 154–159).

A perfectly flat plate can cause an optical illusion, appearing warped or humped up in the middle. At any rate, the flat plate is a hangover from the culinary age of steak, potatoes, and rolling peas. Plates and platters with a bit of depth to them suit our eclectic, contemporary food tastes. A slight curve, an elevation to the rim, or simply a compelling gesture helps keep the form taut.

Keep in mind how an object made of clay retains its shape. The flat mineral particles become aligned and layered with water in a tremendous ionic bond. Think of it as a ring of people holding hands and spinning round and round. As long as everyone holds on tight the ring can spread and flare, but should one person let loose, the whole thing snaps apart. Sometimes pots can still stand, but they look flaccid, as though the particles got tired and lost their grip.

It takes a potter truly dedicated to utility to make a simple plate that will be decorated only by the food it presents. Flat shapes are hard but seldom fun to throw unless they are a large tour de force. The pleasure lies in decorating the uninterrupted space, even if it will be hidden by food.

Clary Illian

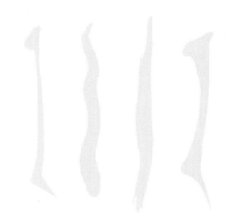

Pots with Lids

By now you are probably eager for the assignments of more complex pots such as covered jars, casseroles, and teapots. But all you need to know about these types of pots is embedded in the exercises you have already completed. Success stems from keen observation and clear decisions.

For example, good storage jars require roomy and accessible interior volumes with lids shaped to respond to the visuals already established. Let's start with a simple cylinder again. A cylinder could be the basis for canisters for flour, sugar, beans, and pasta (figures 160–163). There will not be a "perfect" lid, just different lids telling different visual stories.

Three types of lids are shown: overhanging lids, cap lids, and drop-in lids that require a seat in the rim of the cylinder (figure 164). The cap lid and the drop-in lid simply continue and terminate the lines of the pot. The overhanging lid introduces new dynamics to the form. Although it could simply be a flat pancake closing the opening, it has the potential to be a complex form with height, width, and depth. Completely flat overhanging lids lack the dynamic tension of a hollow shape and call to mind metal or wood. Stepped levels, curved domes modulating at the circumference into an S curve, flat planes, and pitched or curved roofs with attic room underneath are just some of the many options (figure 165). Furthermore, lids offer many opportunities for decorative details repeating elements present in the jar.

The outer edge of the overhanging lid carries a lot of information. Since the rim of the jar isn't visible, the edge tells you about the characteristic thickness of the pot and the mood of the pot. Is it graceful

160

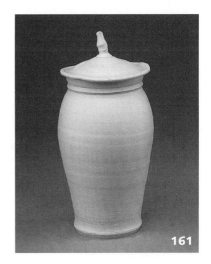

161

162

or sturdy? This edge needs to relate to the pot not only in thickness but in shape. Will it be square or round? Will it taper inward or flare out? Lids are usually made upside down on the wheel, so it is important to think through the eventual placement on the pot. A common error is to unconsciously cup the flange so the edge decision cannot be seen from the typical viewing angle for a pot. Cupping the flange also cuts off the view of the full height of the body of the pot (figures 166, 167).

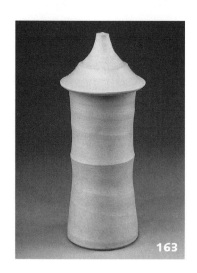

163

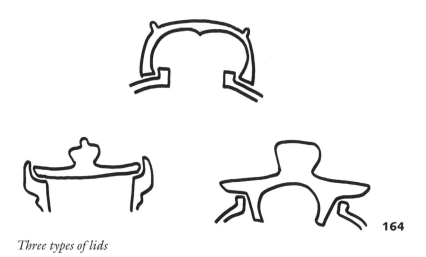

164

Three types of lids

165

Overhanging lids

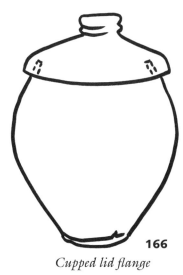

166

Cupped lid flange

167

Corrected lid flange

Although the lost portion of the vertical profile might not be important in a cylinder, it becomes crucial when convex forms are being explored. A cupped overhang chokes the full expression of the curve. A jar with convex curves usually calls for a lid that continues the movement of the walls. The dome of the lid picks up that movement, and the flange offers a plane or curve to relate to some other part of the pot. If the edge of a lid curves in such a way that it moves the gaze down to the ground without reinvolving it with the shape of the pot, it can appear oversized and diminish the pot itself. Since covered jars often please us by the elevation of their volume, downward movement works counter to that pleasure.

Although the overhanging lid obscures part of the form, the degree of shadow it casts is also an important part of the composition. Because pottery is so rich in color and texture, we may neglect the role of the interaction of light with three-dimensional form. Beveled undercuts at the vessel's base, projecting ridges, rims, and lids all make shadows. The undersides of handles, curves, and knobs react differently with light than the top sides and can present a single contrasting dark focal point or the rhythmic repetitions of shadows (figures 168, 169).

168

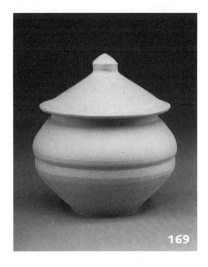

169

170

171

Rooflike overhanging lids often succeed because they have substantial volume of their own, acting like the top half of the total shape (figures 170, 171). The space under the lid can be useful or not, depending upon what you are going to put in the pot. Cap lids have a similar dynamic if they continue a form, but as discrete shapes they can add a whole fashion statement: squatting like a beret, perching like a Jackie Kennedy pillbox hat, or lending to the pot the authority of a bishop's miter (figure 172–174).

Drop-in lids also vary in shape and respond in different ways to the body of the pot (figure 175). They can sink into the form, continue a curve, or make a horizontal termination (figures 176–178).

A few words about lid fit. Drop-in lids need to fit nearly perfectly or the gap will be distracting to the visuals of the pot (figure 179). This is even truer of cap lids that continue the profile of the pot (figure 162). Overhanging lids are a bit more forgiving. In fact, some free play is advisable in case of warpage. The depending ring of clay that slips into the mouth of the jar can slant inward, so only the contact point needs to fit (figure 164).

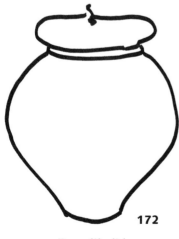

172

Beret-like lid

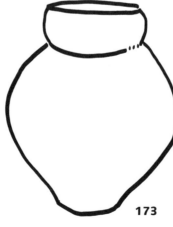

173

Pillbox lid

174

Bishop's miter lid

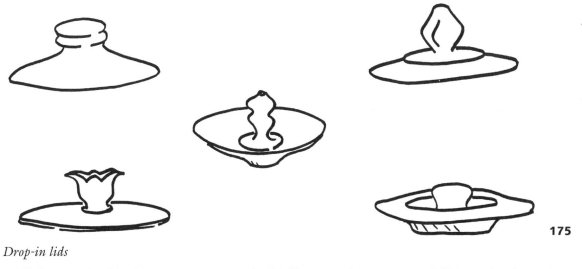

175

Drop-in lids

176

177

178

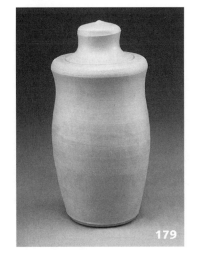

179

180

181

Knobs or no knobs? Knobs aren't mandatory on overhanging lids; many storage pots are complete without them. If overhanging or cap lids are small they can be easily grasped by the edges with one hand, and even larger lids can be lifted with both hands. I know customers prefer lids with knobs, but that shouldn't be the only reason for doing them. If a pot really sings with a plain lid, it simply means you are going to have to reeducate the potential buyer.

It is hard to make a good knob, not so much from the standpoint of function but from the standpoint of freshness. Often the secondary parts of a shape, the handles, knobs, and lugs, kill a pot otherwise uniquely interpreted. Students need to understand that a knob is not just a generic item but, in effect, a tiny pot, and tiny pots deserve just as much attention and respect as bigger pots. The generic knob of choice is shown in figure 180. A few pots are well served by it; most are not. A knob should be consistent in mood and carry the same formal concerns as the rest of the pot (figures 181–184). It can repeat shapes and lines of motion, edge qualities, and surface treatments.

Try throwing as many kinds of knobs as you can. Work off the hump. Make them to the point of boredom and beyond (figures 185–190). Make as many pulled, rolled, squeezed, cut, and constructed handles as you can bear to make (figures 191–196). The more playful your approach, the more success you will have. Think of them as little sculptures. Many times I have discovered a new version of a knob, fallen in love with it, and made months' worth of pots just to do that knob another time.

182

183

184

185–190

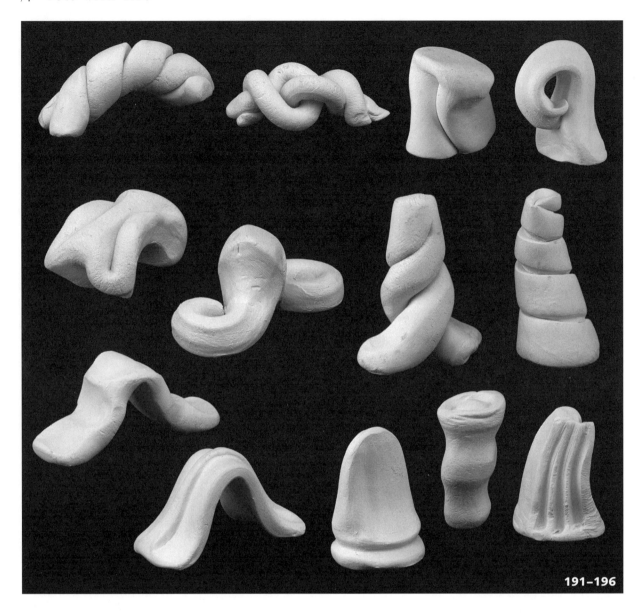

191–196

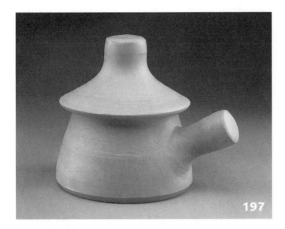

Casseroles

Casseroles are covered pots, sometimes squat cylinders, sometimes turned bowls. Besides the requirements for shallowness and easily accessible cooking space, they are a pot with fewer rules than you might imagine. But you must take into account how they will be carried when hot. Unless there is a generously undercut curve to cradle in the hands with gloves or potholders, you will have to invent lugs that either harmonize with the form or become an interesting contrasting feature.

Lids for wide-mouthed forms often require as much clay as the pot itself. They cannot be too flat or they will sag. If the lid is overhanging, it will have to work well both visually and functionally with the lugs. Knobs must be large enough to be grasped through a potholder (figures 197–200).

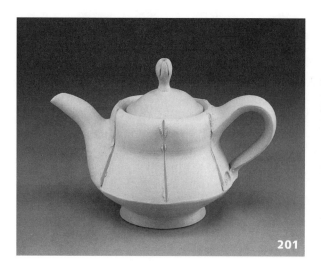

Teapots

Teapots are covered pots with so many parts and pieces that they are beyond the reach of most beginning potters. This is cruel because they are such a seductive form, packed with potent personality and cozy symbolism. I have heard it said that the parts and pieces must not call attention to themselves but be subsumed into a unifying harmony (figures 201, 202). There is also another kind of teapot made just to give expression to a particularly impudent spout, eccentric knob, or flamboyant handle (figures 203, 204). You must decide what the teapot is about beyond mere function—what formal ideas will it convey?

Spouts are usually thrown off the hump, and it is helpful to remember to open the center hole deeper than the cutoff level. This is true for thrown handles as well (figure 205). You cannot easily compress and shape solid clay. Once again, there are no rules for the shape, only conditions that will make it harder or easier to accomplish your goals. You will want to have a very clear notion about the relationship of the spout to the body. Will the spout flow from the body in an uninterrupted curve or is it an articulated shape complicating the profile (figures 206, 207)?

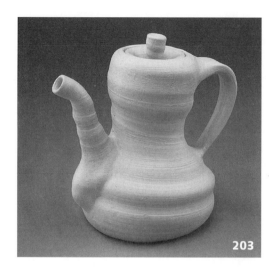

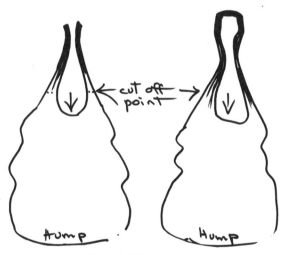

Spout and handle cut off level

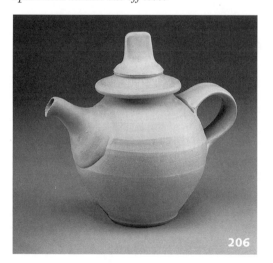

208

The placement and angle of the spout are determined not only by formal concerns but by the level of the tea in a full pot (figure 208). A sharp edge is necessary for dripless pouring. Teapot handles can be placed over the top, to the side, or to the back of the form (figures 209–212). Side and back handles, in particular, introduce horizontal and diagonal movements as they relate to the rest of the parts of the pot. Because of this complexity the teapot is one of the shapes most likely to become artistic statements divorced from use, ideas about teapots rather than teapots themselves.

Covered pots are the true workhorses of ceramics. Even a pitcher becomes more useful when a lid is added. And, like workhorses, they may sacrifice elegance to utility. The narrow mouths of spherical jars, teapots, and narrow-necked pitchers create beautiful forms at the expense of ease of access and cleaning. It is a challenge to make them both exciting and easy to use.

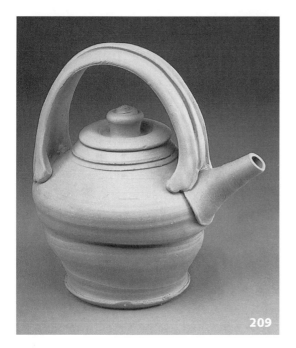

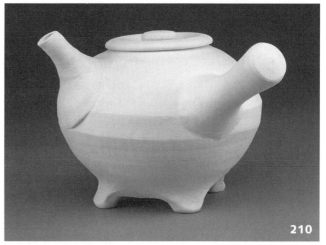

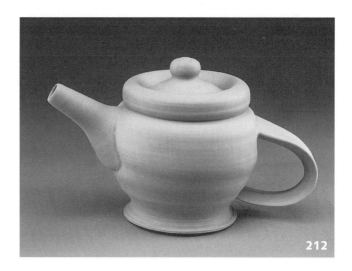

Learning to See

You won't like this exercise. You will think it designed to kill your creativity, frustrate you, or bore you to tears. Take two pounds of clay and make the shape shown in figure 213. The intention is not to challenge your throwing skills so much as your seeing skills.

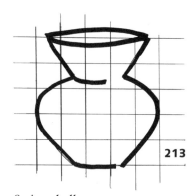

213

Seeing challenge

Here are some pots made in response to this exercise (figures 214–217). Assuming the potters put the clay exactly where they wanted it, the pots still fail to duplicate the required shape in one way or another. The reason is a lack of attention to details. Using the grid helps you see the details. It shows the relationship of height to width and the relationship of the parts to one another. It shows the outermost thrust of the belly occurring midway on the bottom section of the pot, which is made up of a curve rolling in at the shoulder but flattening as it flows to the base. It also makes clear the similar diameter of rim and belly, base, and neck.

Notice that the schematic drawing shows a slightly elevated view of the pot rather than a true profile. It is rare to look at or to live with pots in true profile, and, for that matter, potter's wheels do not allow the maker to view profiles easily because the upper body is usually placed above the work to facilitate throwing. In spite of all this, potters still make judgments from true profile. Like the distorted figures on a Italian Renaissance chapel ceiling, a pot needs to be exaggerated in some of its aspects to create the desired impression when seen from a typical angle.

Analyzing a pot by placing it on a grid is excessive, but you will want to acquire the skill of accurate observation by some means. Try to develop a sort of mental grid, an awareness of where every square inch

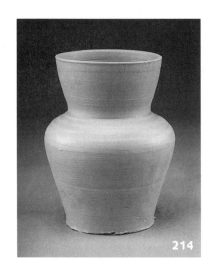

214

of the pot is placed. Even if you have no desire to repeat identical shapes or to copy pots you admire, you need to be able to produce the pots you have imagined in your mind's eye. Visualizations are more than just feelings, though they may begin in that way; they are most helpful if they are fairly detailed. Even if you prefer spontaneous and intuitive improvisation on the wheel as a way to generate ideas, you still need to see accurately in order to make decisions on a moment-to-moment basis. In time you will want to succeed intentionally rather than by happy accident.

Unfortunately, repetition and replication are the most efficient methods for learning to see. Comparing one pot to another and another and yet another of the same shape shows you what you are doing right or wrong. The added bonus is that you are also gaining hand/eye coordination. Repetition throwing is controversial in the modern studio pottery movement. The great fear is that the pots will lose vitality due to routinized throwing. Advocates of this approach feel the economy of movement that results from repeating shapes is directly responsible for an enlivened surface and elastic curves. They see the challenge grow with each repetition. The point where pleasurable competence fades into dutiful performance is different for each person.

You can also train your eye by making a group of similar but not identical pots, lining them up, and studying them. When you do this, not only will you see deviations from the prototype, but you will also begin to draw conclusions about comparative success and failure of the interaction of the parts. This is seeing of a different order. Bernard Leach believed that a group of people with trained eyes would be able to agree on which pots work the best. I have found that in group critiques it is easy for everyone to spot the failures, but personal taste often enters into the attempt to pick the winners.

All of the eye-training scenarios discussed so far could be misinterpreted as suggesting a fixed point of view, as though pots were two-dimensional. Pots must be viewed from all directions to reveal their full nature. Philip Rawson describes the principles of quality governing thrown pottery form in this way. He observes that since a perfect circle is what the potter's wheel produces inevitably at any point as the clay passes through the hands as seen from above, a pot is more expressive of the plastic nature of clay and the maker's intervention when the profile is not a perfect circle. He recommends taking a pot, looking into its mouth, and then rotating it through a full circle, keeping the

215

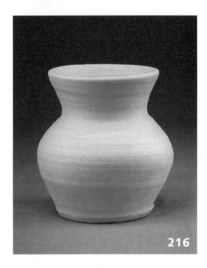

216

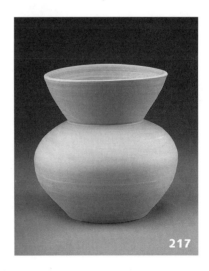

217

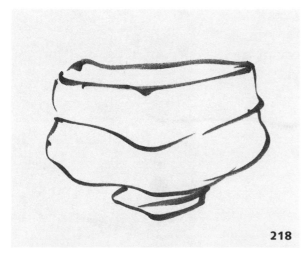

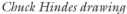

Chuck Hindes drawing

Chuck Hindes teabowl

opening always at right angles to your body. Look at the contour as it moves through a complete rotation and notice how it changes. It should change subtly and continually, he says, to convey vitality.[1]

Drawing the shape you wish to make can firm up your intentions and offer another base of comparison. It is important that the scale be large enough to demand lively firm lines and decision making about all the contours of the pot. Tiny diagrams just will not do the job. For example, the drawing at the beginning of the chapter only shows proportions and could not help the maker inform the pot with any other characteristics. Pottery students often are very reluctant to draw. It seems to be the ceramic equivalent of being asked to sing in front of the class. But there is no doubt that drawing trains the eye and the hand, and the ability to lay a line on paper directly abets the ability to lay up a line of clay in space. It may take awhile to find the drawing tool that best suits your hand and best captures your touch with clay. As you notice a particular quality in the drawings, attempt to duplicate it in clay. It is even possible that drawing could lead the development of personal interpretation (figures 218, 219).

Language can help you learn to see. All of this book is language about form, and the assignments have been a systematic naming of the parts of form and their relationships. If naming draws close attention, that attention will surely help you to see. The more precise and vivid the naming, the more memorable it is as an aid. I was once told that someone found a bowl of mine "grave and charming." Those adjectives hit with the familiar thud of unexpectedly seeing myself in a mirror and gave me a more focused concept of the mood I want to capture in my pots.

The virtue in precise descriptive language is the absence of built-in value judgment traps. Woodworker David Pye names all the characteristics of manufactured objects. So thorough and well organized is his catalog of visual possibilities that he creates a sort of zip-code map of manufactured things. Using this map one can then send each object to its proper destination without getting into arguments about whether New York is better than rural Tennessee or Florida better than Massachusetts. Each place has its qualities which can then be discussed on their merits.

Metaphor is a powerful language tool. Janet Koplos once wrote in a review that jars "flexed their shoulders." [2] Arthur Danto has described an imaginary culture in which "the pots have a certain squat elegance, and their smooth sides strike out from the base in a daring curve, and then curve back sharply, as if in emulation of the trajectory of a marvelous bird." [3]

Most provocative of the uses of language are questions. What qualities do you want that pot to convey? Energy? What kind of energy: agitated energy, exuberant energy, or hovering energy? What components of the pot contribute to the impression of agitation, exuberance, or hovering? Why? Behind every answer lies another question.

Training the eye is more than a matter of practice; the real problem is to get your mind or assumptions out of the way. Intention and execution are not identical. The task of seeing what is really there rather than what you hope is there is a discipline of almost spiritual proportions. You must be absolutely in the moment with no attachment to preconceived notions in order to see objectively.

What you will see are curves, angles, and proportions that are not correct in themselves but, in Gregory Bateson's words, are "primarily a dance of interconnecting parts . . . only secondarily pegged down by various physical limits." [4] Success lies in how the parts are combined, and different combinations can be equally successful. Bateson was writing about the morphology of plants and animals, but the potter feels a powerful connection to his words.

To compare pots to living organisms may seem to be stretching it a bit, but there are many shared qualities between the two. Pots and animals share axial symmetry and segmentation; their parts are repetitive and rhythmical. Both are containers of sorts, their skins wrapping around their vital parts: muscles, skeletons, and organs in the case of animals and the volume for food, drink, and flowers in the case of pots. Both grow by unfolding from a center point over time. Both must follow certain principles of movement as they respond to the forces of nature.

It is intriguing to learn that the spiraling growth of a pot on the wheel is a pattern made, with few exceptions, only by living things. Bateson goes on to say that "all symmetry and segmentation [are] somehow a result of, a payoff from, the fact of growth; and that growth makes its formal demands. A thing is aesthetic because it is responsive to the pattern which connects."[5] We all have access to this logic on an intuitive level, and it could explain Leach's idea that quality judgments in pottery can be objective rather than purely subjective.

György Doczi puts it this way: "The Art as well as the wisdom and knowledge of East and West alike testify that there exists a deep-rooted unity below the many surface diversities of this world. This unity manifests itself in simple proportional relationships that create patterns of harmonious wholeness out of the vast and dinergetically opposed diversities in nature, in the arts, and at times in the arts of living."[6] Dinergy is the pattern-generating power of two forces acting upon an object at the same time. Making pots is a perfect example of dinergy: the revolving wheel is one force, the potter's shaping hands are another. Doczi's book *The Power of Limits* contains fascinating analyses of the proportional relationships of natural objects and manufactured objects, including pots, that show the consistencies in the way things are organized.

Can the potter find guidelines in these consistencies? The proportions of three-dimensional objects are comprehended in many different ways. The relationship of height to width is only the beginning. The contours of pots modulate from simple to very complex planes and curves, sometimes even breaking the form into two or more discrete units. Additionally, it is the intangible volumes, the space inside, that we ultimately want to bring into speaking relationship.

I chose the shape you were asked to duplicate because I thought its 1:1 relationship of height to width and simple shape would be easy to keep in mind while throwing. I was convinced that it would be a static shape because of this proportional parity, but I hadn't taken into account how the division of the form into two units, a swelling belly tightly reined in by a flaring neck, would energize that basic proportion.

Would the pot be better if the relationship of height to width were 1:2 or 3:4? Neither of these changes produce a better pot. What happens if these ratios describe the relationship between the two parts of the pot rather than simply between the overall height to width? Neither of these changes produces a better pot, only a different pot.

One proportional relationship that has been held forth as desirable in the past is the ratio of 2:3. The golden ratio is created when a line is divided into two segments in such a way that the longest segment divided by the shortest segment equals 1.6. If line segments divided in this way describe the sides of a rectangle, it is a golden rectangle with proportions of 5:8. An approximation of 2:3 is close enough for the craftsperson's purposes. Doczi says, "This is . . . a uniquely reciprocal relationship between two unequal parts of a whole, in which the smallest part stands in the same proportion to the larger part as the large part stands to the whole. The power of the golden section to create harmony arises from its capacity to unite the different parts of a whole so that each preserves its own identity, and yet blends into the greater pattern of a single whole"[7] (figure 220).

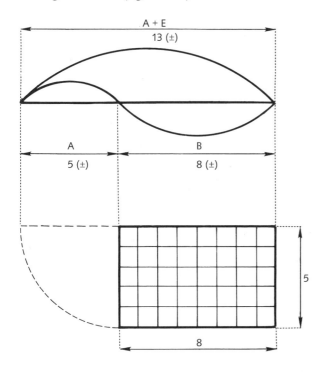

A : B = B : (A + B) = 0.618...   B : A = (A + B) : B = 1.618...

5 : 8 = 0.625; 8 : 13 = 0.615   8 : 5 = 1.6; 13 : 8 = 1.62   **220**
Golden section and golden rectangle

Proportional relationships also govern the unfurling of curves. A curve that is simply a segment of a circle exhibits no dynamism. A curve whose journey picks up the pace, tightening the arc at one end or another, begins to spiral. If a spiral is based on the pattern of squares that can be constructed within the golden rectangle, it is called the golden spiral (figure 221).

Doczi describes another pattern-forming process shared by music, color, light, and anatomy. This is called harmonic progression, "a series of fractions in which the nominator remains 1 while all neighboring denominators share the same difference, e.g. 1/1, 1/1.2, 1/1.4, 1/1.6, 1/1.8."[8] This process would be dizzyingly difficult to use in the making of shapes, but it might become a conscious tool in the repetition of similar decorative elements. To put it more simply, rather than dividing a form into equal parts, create interest and movement by placing those divisions progressively farther and farther apart (figure 222).

Familiarity with the golden rectangle and the golden spiral is basic to the educated potter not only because they provide the inevitable underpinnings of objects but because so much art from the past was consciously based upon them. Such deliberation and faith in a comprehensibly ordered universe are not part of our times. No one looks at or makes pots with diagrams of the golden section or golden spiral in mind. Only the simplest proportional relationships can be held consciously in the mind as we make decisions about shapes.

Although the knowledge that predictable proportional relationships govern the organization of form is thrilling, the received language of

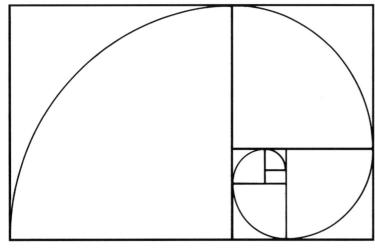

221

Golden spiral

form particular to each culture and each age probably includes a characteristic shift in the underlying mathematics. Our fascination with these pots and our sense of wonder might stem from the mystery of this unfamiliar shift. The roots of form become matters of fashion and style and finally individual interpretation.

If proportions are not right or wrong in themselves, why do students ask if a foot is too narrow or a neck too short? Look back at the gridded drawing (figure 213). The pot that achieved the most accurate rendering also has clean lines. There is no lumpiness or wavering at the base, no wishy-washiness in the crisp definition between the plane of the neck and the curve of the body (figure 223). We respond to a quality of clear assertion, whatever the proportions.

Each pot has within it a logic that, if followed, leads to success. The foot that is too narrow is a foot that is not responding to the rest of the pot. The solution might be a slight flattening of the curve of the bowl as it reaches to meet the foot, or the same narrow foot angled 5 degrees differently. The stunted neck may not need more height but more meat. As Bateson says, it is a dance of interconnecting parts.

The most intriguing pot made in response to the assignment has a thick, flat rim edge that creates a shadow pulling the eye into the pot and creating a curved surface on the inside of the neck to contrast with the flat plane of its outside surface. It is only a small variation on the theme, but what an immense and pleasurable difference it makes (figure 224).

Inconsistency beween what is suggested and what is actually manifested, hesistation in a plane or a curve, vagueness at the beginnings and endings of all the parts of a pot—these are just some of the failings that might give the viewer the sense that something is wrong. Pots will succeed to the extent that a dialogue takes place between the shape and all of the other parts of the form: the volume, material, surface, thickness and shapes in the walls, interaction with light, rhythms, scale, architectural detailing, and (let's not forget) use.

These seeing tools are analytical and involve breaking form down into its constituent parts, an activity with a bad reputation among artists. Many believe analysis has no place in the creative act. Learning how to see does not insure creativity. The magical moments when you take wing and fly from a familiar land to an unknown place are a gift. But you can ready yourself for the receipt and use of that gift by learning how to see with every tool at your command.

222

Harmonic progression

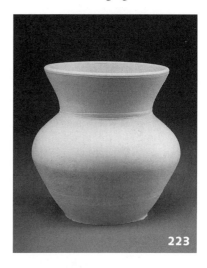

223

224

Style and Voice

Learning about utilitarian form is only part of the battle for excellence. You must also develop a personal style. In fact, from the beginning you have unwittingly been developing style; you could hardly avoid it since each person handles clay in a different way and has different inherent preferences. Your style has been evident in everything you have done so far. The assignment now is to bring everything you have made together in one place and try to characterize it. Develop a list of questions to help put words to what you are seeing.

I remember when Leach called my attention to the fact that I was developing a characteristic convex curve. I thought it was the same curve all my fellow apprentices were pursuing, but he could see the minute changes of dynamic in my execution of the curve. I suppose many traits in my work were identifiable: the increments chosen for rims and undercut bevels, the exact shape of an edge, or the rhythms of gesture. We apprentices at the Leach Pottery could always tell who had made a piece even though we made standardized pots completely dictated in weight and silhouette by the catalog.

The previous assignments in this book have been calculated to bring all the decisions you have to make while forming a pot to the conscious level and to broaden your repertoire. You should be open to trying everything without fear that something unique to you will be destroyed; be confident that your style is evolving on its own. Only when you completely understand your options, are able to see accurately, and can perceive the logic of structure is it time to consider style.

It is possible that personal style, like popularity, cannot be achieved intentionally. In fact, approaching style directly is probably a bad idea.

Style is a means to an end, not an end in itself. The important thing is to have fascinations, preferences, nagging questions, enthusiasms, and, finally, passions. Noticing your concerns and continually defining and refining them is what gives birth to personal style. Advanced students are frequently worried about the presence of two or three different stylistic approaches in their work. If each of these styles is prompted by strong attraction and the desire to work something out, this diversity is only a problem of time, energy, and focus, not a fault.

Because, as I have explained, pottery form is a received language, it is, perhaps, more accurate to say that a potter gravitates toward an already established style and then must strive to give it a personal voicing. Styles (or perhaps you could call them schools of utilitarian pottery) are cumulative accretions of shared visuals, usually created by many people working in the same manner. Occasionally the improvisations of a potter working in a recognized school are so outstanding that imitations pop up, and a new style is born. New styles can also be sparked by the synthesis of previously distinct looks. In the past, new styles were often provoked by a technical discovery such as shared materials and kilns.

There is no shame in participating in an established style. This is the way it has worked throughout the history of the craft, but only in modern times has the choice of a style become a matter of affinity rather than birthright. It is still a communal affair, even though the bond is no longer determined by geography but by attraction. Acknowledging participation is also acknowledging that the order of creativity involved is one of interpretation rather than composition, and this contributes to clarity of thinking on the part of everyone involved.

The line between participating in a style and copying the unique voicing of a fellow potter is murky. Shapes, materials, and firing methods are the generic concerns of a group of practitioners, but such details as a signature gesture, the particular articulation of the end of a handle, or an idiosyncratic tweaking of proportions and scale are the trademark solutions of an individual. Once you are aware of this difference, you should fight the impulse to copy and challenge yourself to find new solutions.

Thirty-five years ago the prevailing look of utilitarian pottery in the United States was influenced by Scandinavian and German contemporary craft and craftspersons who had immigrated to this country. Although the potters involved looked admiringly toward the pots of

James McKinnell

the East, their interests were limited to the shapes of the various classical periods. The work itself featured crisp lines, staccato gestures or smooth surfaces, high-fire matte glazes, and angular rim shapes and edges (figures 225–227). Now these pots look linear in their structural conceptions, and the decoration seems dated because it owed more to the popular design fashions of the time than to a searching exploration of pattern or imagery.

The work from this period celebrates the fired properties of clay, its stoniness and strength rather than its wet and tactile qualities. These potters laid a strong groundwork of technical exploration, scholarship, and a dedication to craftsmanship that set off an explosion of activity and styles.

Much has been written about the innovative work of Peter Volkos and his various students and associates on the West Coast during the late 1950s. They invented a new kind of ccramics using the vessel as a departure point for artistic exploration in terms of the formal concerns of the high art of the period. They were no longer making utilitarian pottery, but the energetic and spontaneous way they handled clay influenced people who still wished to remain within the limitations of utility. A funkier, more luscious, more loosely gestured sensibility started to emerge, a sensibility that exploited the wet qualities of clay. The scale of the work grew as utilitarian potters tried to reclaim attention in an increasingly complex craft scene. Three storage jars by Ken Ferguson dating from 1978 to 1998 perfectly demonstrate this exploratory evolution (figures 228–230).

James McKinnell

Bunny McBride

Kenneth Ferguson

Kenneth Ferguson

Kenneth Ferguson

As the study of ceramics lodged more and more firmly in academia and the emphasis changed to embrace the tenets of modernism, there was more and more emphasis on experimentation and individuation. The utilitarian potters, by then a subcategory in the field, responded with work romantic in its impulse toward exaggeration, asymmetry, expressiveness, and dominance of the parts over the whole (figures 231, 232). Classical ideals of harmony, symmetry, restraint, and dominance of the whole over the parts fell out of favor.

Vibrant color and low-fired clay bodies were relegitimized. Raku enjoyed a brief vogue, although it is unsuitable for a wide range of utilitarian items. A discernible style was developed by people using red clay bodies and colorful brushwork on white majolica glazes. The shapes were often very playful, but the thrown surface was uninflected to allow for fluid brushwork (figures 233, 234).

Chris Staley

Peter Beasecker

233

234

Linda Arbuckle   *Stanley Andersen*

Warren MacKenzie

In Minnesota Warren MacKenzie, a Leach-trained potter, was making strong pots representing another visual possibility. His work owed much to the folk pots of Japan, Korea, and China with their traditional *tenmoku*, *shino*, and oatmeal glazes and simple direct throwing. Some of his students had apprenticeships in Japan, where they used wood kilns for the first time. They altered thrown shapes into squares, rectangles, and diamonds and decorated the austere surfaces of unglazed wood-fired clay with simple brush strokes. This group influenced many devotees, most of them dedicated to making modestly sized pots for everyday use (figures 235–239)

Randy Johnston

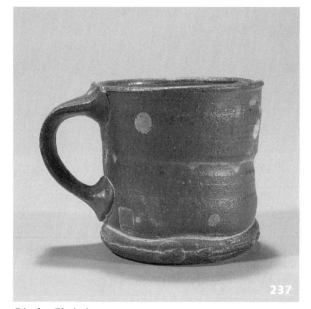

Linda Christianson

Michael Simon

Wayne Branum

David Shaner

Jim Lorio

Wood firing, particularly in *anagama* or *noborigama* kilns, is currently experiencing a tremendous popularity. Not surprisingly, wood firers often look to the East for models upon which to base their work, and a group of potters are making work like the unglazed storage jars, teapots, and vases of the great folk kilns of Japan (figures 240–243). Wood kilns are pot gobblers, their sheer size demanding a level of production that is good news for the utilitarian pot. The revival of this style, emphasizing as it does the accidental beauty of natural processes, vividly expresses reaction to slick contemporary objects.

The most recent approach to utilitarian pots to emerge as a discernible style emphasizes altering, cutting, and reassembling wheel-thrown pieces to achieve complicated shapes with asymmetrical stance and great animation. These pots often feature lyrical horizontal and diagonal movement. Because they are labor intensive, they are more expensive and tend to push away from casual everyday use into more ceremonial functions. They express the high values our society assigns to individuality and ingenuity in the arts (figures 244–247).

Almost all the styles enjoying critical acclaim in the last twenty years have featured a deft, relaxed kind of throwing with noticeable gesture and irregular profiles. Students feeling the pressure of this fashion often ask how to make their pots look looser. The look can come only

Rob Barnard

Chuck Hindes

Jeff Oestreich

Peter Beasecker

Josh DeWeese

Kris Nelson

from the process, and so the simple answer to this question is to throw with great economy of movement on a slow-turning wheel. A better answer deals with the implicit value judgment of the question.

Although they may be out of fashion, pots made with controlled perfection of proportion, elegance of line, and absence of gestural variation are not bad in themselves. *Tightness* and *looseness*, the terms commonly used to describe these two manners of working, are only options. They occupy different positions on the continuum from freedom to regulation in workmanship devised by David Pye.[1] The wheel is a shape-determining system, but it allows variations in the shape and rhythms of surface gestures that in turn modulate the profile. The gestures also participate in the proportional relationships of the whole pot.

Loose pots exploit the interaction between the shape and the movements that make it. A loose gesture can be so spacious and vigorous that it divides the shape into distinct parts, perhaps even changing the underlying geometry. A subtler gesture can introduce small rhythms, barely noticeable but instrumental in reiterating the broader themes of the pot. Loosely gestured pots are forgiving in profile and proportion.

Tight pots with little or no gesture suggest a mode of perfection and the pursuit of ideal shapes and so depend more upon the elegance of their proportions. The surface interest is created by glaze or decoration. Although highly regulated pots are not the fashion just now, they are a valid option (fiture 248). Whether loose or tight, what is important is a consistency of intention and effect.

Peter Pinnell

The purpose of this summary of the history of the modern studio movement is to support the notion that communally developed styles are still the engine driving pottery. Each loosely defined style still has disciples who find in it meaning and nurturance. For example, when ceramics became identified with academia, it split into a market-based branch and a status-based branch. The market, more hospitable to the stoneware vessels of the 1950s, has encouraged the making of similar work for decades. Raku has endured in the same fashion. Potters seeking personal voicings have combined styles. These mixtures become discrete styles and, in turn, attract disciples of their own.

It is important to know where your work stands in the scheme of things because that knowledge pushes you toward growth. Knowing you work within a style enables you to recognize your sources and move to a more deeply researched and personally experienced body of work. Look beyond the work of contemporary potters to the sources they use. When you follow this river upstream, you will come to springs that well up from the whole world of manufactured and natural objects. You will learn what moves you at the deepest level.

Finally, the subject of your exploring gaze will be yourself: your idiosyncratic way of handling clay, your characteristic formal choices, and the moods your pots create and the stories they tell. Whether this results in a clear voicing within an established style or something new that stands on its own, only time will tell.

Utility and Tradition

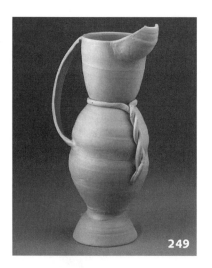

249

250

Potters fall into the belief that an ideal shape can be discovered for each useful category, but this is not true. There are surprisingly few rules on the subject of utility. A sincere dedication to utility and desire for certainty has caused this misinterpretation of the familiar phrase "form follows function." [1] A potter once told me she had been taught that every bowl should flare out at the rim. This was supposed to make it easy to hold. While it sounds logical, pleasurable experiences with bowls shaped differently suggest that this rule is too limiting.

The assignment is to make an assortment of bowl shapes of different proportions and turn them into pouring vessels. You can use any process; you can add or subtract. Get crazy! Figures 249–252 show some innovative responses to this assignment. Notice the terrific variety of shapes. Their makers are no longer depending upon generic solutions but are thinking creatively about the basic volumes and functions of a pouring vessel.

Notions about utility, far from being objective truths, are as subjective as notions of taste. In fact, subjectivity is appropriate because each person has a unique way of handling pots and unique functional needs. People develop habits of using objects based on individual strength, dexterity, experience, and concepts about the meanings of objects in their intimate environment. One person, for example, might claim that pottery is more ideally useful the lighter it is. Another person could find these same light pots insubstantial and vulnerable. When I reach into the cupboard for a bowl, I usually choose an open shape, finding it more inviting, but a friend always opts for bowls with en-

closing shapes with broad feet because she wants stability. My prefer-
ence must be subjective.

If it is not true that only one shape can fit a purpose, surely it is true
that whatever the shape, it should work. For example, spouts should
pour without making a mess, casseroles should not collect food in
tight corners, and knobs should not slip out of your fingers. This is
the true dialogue of utility, but to all of these requirements there are
many solutions. In addition, both makers and users have a range of
tolerance for how perfectly the solutions must work. It is odd that
the criteria of certainty and regulation that govern the appearance of
machine-made objects are presumed to govern their utilitarian design.
Think how messy a plastic milk jug is, how hard to tilt when full. This
assumption, however incorrect, informs our standards of utility much
as the appearance of machine-made objects has informed the standards
of appearance.

Potters differ in how directly they deal with the subject of utility.
For some, specific utilitarian requirements are a great source of ideas,
spawning such objects as thrown and altered fish platters; a stack of
forms that breaks down into a cup, saucer, and Melitta-style filter; or

Betty Woodman teaset

compartmented serving pieces for finger foods (figures 253–256). The assignment of this chapter teaches the pleasure of approaching design from this angle.

For others, utility is simply a given aspect of the making of generic shapes such as pitchers, bowls, and mugs while the ideas sprout from purely formal concerns. These potters fall in love with a curve or discover a new way of treating a terminating edge and investigate the manifestations of these visual themes in different utilitarian settings.

Whatever the route to improvisation, as long as the parameters are direct and economical use of the wheel and utilitarian intention, the pots are apt to look like pots you've seen before. It is not possible to invent a new shape, but only in the twentieth century has this become a reason for denial and shame. György Doczi suggests, "Perhaps, in our fascination with our own powers of invention and achievement, we have lost sight of the power of limits . . . limitations are not just restrictive, they are creative."[2]

Nevertheless, the shapes we cannot invent anew we can interpret anew. Utilitarian pots made on the wheel carry on a dialogue with tradition, and the interpretations of already known forms are greater

Kris Nelson coffee set

Steve Davis-Rosenbaum chip and dip bowl

Josh DeWeese oil and vinegar

than the sum of their parts. We take pleasure in a solid foundation of familiarity and are enabled by it to see and take pleasure in the layer of improvisation.

When I began trying to sell pottery in rural Iowa thirty years ago, few of my customers had seen contemporary wheel-thrown pots and often asked if they were antiques. Perhaps they were responding unconsciously to the look of materials touched by human hands. Perhaps they remembered seeing older pots in the homes of their grandparents. Because of my great admiration for the pots of the past, I was flattered. I knew my pots were not simply replicas but reinterpretations of generic forms.

Place

I received an inheritance of incomparable value from my experience at the Leach Pottery in 1964 and 1965. It included a standard of excellence, a coherent received language of form, a place in the world of handmade ceramics, and the model of a working life in a production pottery. Although it was established in 1920 and clearly incorporated the reactionary stance of the Arts and Crafts Movement, it had real ties to folk pottery practice from the past. We apprentices felt personally connected to an unbroken tradition.

This sense of identification may have been historically naive, but it has served me well, giving me the momentum, clarity, and commitment to succeed as an independent potter with a vision of the kind of pots I want to make. It has also given me some strong feelings about Stravinsky's phrase "the reality of what endures," the meanings that pots can carry.

As potters search for aesthetic excellence, they assume the lessons learned are communicated by the work. Some of those are the lessons of perception: the ability to see what is really there, to see the diversity and individuality in each piece, to see the workmanship involved in achieving the effects, and to see the underlying relationships and find in them order, vitality, or beauty—that is, to experience them as meaningful in themselves.

Some are lessons of extended meaning and deal with the implications of these perceptions. The discipline of seeing what is really there implies a quieting of the mind and the emotions. Appreciation of workmanship implies standards of human proficiency. Appreciation of individuality, diversity, and order implies respect for the way things work in the natural world. The potter hopes the extended meanings of perception are also carried to the users. This is a tall order for a utilitarian pot.

In his book *A Search for Structure,* Cyril Stanley Smith says, "I believe that the life of the craftsman, indeed of any man making something to be enjoyed and used, is a fine example of what it is to be human: mind, eye, muscle, and hand interacting with the properties of matter to produce shapes reflecting the purposes and cultural values of his society, and sometimes to extending them."[1] Doczi claimed that the underlying proportional harmonies that govern nature and the arts can at times even extend to the arts of living.

Potters occupy a special position as communicators because they straddle the visual arts and the arts of living; they have one foot in the spiritual realm of artistic value judgments and one foot in the material world of utilitarian objects. A useful object that has been crafted with artistic standards in mind is doubly special and celebrates both how and where it will be used. When a customer tells me he must begin the day with coffee from my mug and nothing else will do, I know he has made a ritual. The sensuous appeal of a unique mug is linked to a nurturing moment, a moment of repose before the demands of the day begin. Food, drink, and plants are so central to our daily lives, so charged with emotions of self-gratification, nurturance, and relationship to other human beings that the containers associated with them will always be objects of symbolic power.

Many would have the artist-potter abandon the desire to make affordable domestic ware and aim for a more innovative kind of object making. After all, machines manufacture pottery so much more efficiently and cheaply. "It is very easy to fall into the notion that if the new is viable, then there must have been something wrong with the old."[2] Although the mass production of tablewares gained an important foothold in this country as early as 1825, it has not satisfied our needs on all levels. What else can explain the continuing market for hand-thrown pottery? Abandoning utilitarian vessels to machine production would narrow the range of delight and meaning these objects can carry.

In the last four decades American ceramists have challenged definitions, blurring the boundaries between art and craft. It has been a period of energetic innovation and rising standards of excellence. There have been some grafts onto the tree of ceramics, and every branch has been fruitful. Now is the time to find names for the new hybrid fruits and to revalue the meaning of the term "pottery." Pottery is a word that describes a branch of ceramics, and it is my branch. I'd like to bring back a more limited definition of the word.

Let me begin with the help of an analogy. Wynton Marsalis, jazz and classical trumpet player and educator, has a rather narrow definition of jazz. During an address to the National Press Club on National Public Radio in the fall of 1995, he said that music is jazz only if it is collective improvisation based on the twelve-bar blues progression. When asked how he would classify free jazz, he replied, "It's improvisation, but it's not jazz." He was very clear about this definition but not judgmental. He simply said free jazz is something else. He did not say it is inferior.

I would like to make a similar distinction about the word "pottery." Pottery is a branch of handmade ceramics in which the forms are determined primarily by functional (utilitarian) considerations. Pots, by this definition, should be reasonably easy to use, offer a generous amount of internal space in proportion to the total package of form, and be of a cost that corresponds to their use.

These qualifications are a matter of degree and interpretation, with the limitation of cost being an especially tricky part of the definition. Cost is a word that includes price but is not limited to it. Cost is also the level of effort taken to produce the object. If utility is a primary consideration, it follows that elaborate and time-consuming processes will at some point militate against utility because of the consequent price charged for labor. This definition of utility calls for clear intentions on the part of the maker about the nature of the pots and the target clientele.

There are many kinds of hollow objects made out of clay, and some of them are improvisations on traditional pottery forms, but they are not pottery in the sense that they invite use with food, drink, or plants. They are still useful and valuable just as all art is useful and valuable; that is, they communicate and add meaning to people's lives. All vessels have functions but not necessarily utility. All vessels are not pottery.

Pottery can have all the formal components of the fine arts. Its content or symbolic meaning is unlimited, but it is a category of the arts whose subject is utility. To be classified as pottery a vessel must be in service to the possibility of containing or offering something other than itself. This is the "twelve-bar blues" part of the definition of pottery.

The most problematical aspect of this definition is the position it assigns to the vase. Most potters enjoy making vases they know to be purely decorative and never designed to hold a flower; this is certainly true for me. The prototypes for the shapes come straight from tradition, but the uses they might once have occasioned have dropped away. Many contemporary decorative vases have the shapes of storage vessels, so they are very much about potentially useful space. They point out that the twelve-bar blues of pottery is not utility itself but accessible volume.

The enduring value of wheel-thrown utilitarian pottery resides in a structuring order particularly rich in detail and symbolic content. Utility adds a second layer of meaning. The limitations of structure and utility restrict wheel-thrown pottery to a traditional visual language. Appreciation of tradition is a particularly important lesson in this time of fear and uncertainty when all seems to be in flux. The continuity of using pottery made by an ancient process offers great comfort in our personal lives by affirming values that transcend the moment. David Pye again supplies another key idea: "first of all the things we inherit from the past remind us that the men who made them were like us and give us a tangible link with them. This is a thought to set off against the knowledge that life is short."[3]

Because of my experience as an apprentice, I also have a definition of "pottery" as a place, a worksite tied to production. The word *studio* implies a worksite tied chiefly to the expression of personal artistic exploration. Thinking of "pottery" as a place dedicated to a utilitarian product acknowledges its connection to the community and the responsibility to respond to its needs and at the same time direct those needs through education.

Social critics find a home in this craft. Modern studio pottery practice is still motivated by concerns and ideals first proposed by John Ruskin in 1850 and popularized by William Morris and others in the Arts and Crafts Movement at the end of the last century.[4] Handmade objects are an antidote to a soulless world flooded by products made with a minimum of effort for maximum profit and no reverence for natural materials. A pottery is an alternative to workplaces that are inimical to a worker's need for pleasant conditions and a sense of accomplishment. The life of a potter provides a chance for autonomy and social relevance.

Potters often have social motivations, but that does not guarantee artistic merit. Though they may incorrectly assess their work, they are right about the capacity of good pots to affect the user. Conversely, most potters trained in academic settings have been taught to follow the muse wherever it takes them, allowing their development as artists to determine their niche in the clay community and their relationship to society. A long-held conviction in the art world holds that aesthetic considerations will inevitably be contaminated by contextual considerations. "Politics makes bad art" was an idea universally embraced during the Modernist era, and it still holds sway. When this distrust of social considerations is teamed with the belief also rooted in Modernism (and therefore equally in need of reassessment) that aesthetic pursuits will tend inevitably toward innovation and away from utility, a powerful pressure is created. These attitudes within the art world, not resistance from society at large, push students away from utilitarian pottery.

Students may wish to ignore social interactions and deny the implications of their aesthetic decisions, but pots do not exist in a vacuum. The questions of who makes the work, for whom, how, and why are all there whether the potter wants to deal with them or not. If the artistic statement and processes become so elaborate that they overwhelm utilitarian identity, the maker has made a decision about the role of and the audience for the work. The making of pottery offers a life in the arts in which both quality and social responsibility can be considered.

There can be no doubt: handmade pots are made by privileged people for privileged people. The potter's privilege is not necessarily one of wealth or class but one of education and the freedom to succeed outside of the mainstream. Potters can choose a life dedicated to pursuing excellence and individuation rather than a life given over to surviving. In a sense, they are privileged because they have the luxury of being idealistic. Although it is a struggle to make a living making pots, it is the struggle of any entrepreneur who wants to create a product or service with integrity.

Buyers are even more clearly privileged. They have income to spare for the extras of life. This position of potters and buyers in society presents some contradictions and conflicts. It is especially ironic that the forms of folk pottery once made by the poor for the poor are still the basis for the visual language now perpetuated by an educated group of people for a well-to-do group of people. If the potter believes that pots are good for people, it follows that she will want all "the folks" to have them, not just the rich folks. The widening gap between rich and poor and the heavy expenses of education and starting a business make this desire increasingly unrealistic. How is it possible to reconcile the claim that "a handmade cup can change the world" with the fact that the people involved at both ends of the exchange are found only among the shrinking numbers who benefit from the status quo?[5] This difficult ethical problem has no clear answer, but each potter must take her stand—does take a stand whether consciously or not—through decisions about the product and the price.

A clearer argument can be made that society as a whole benefits from the example of pottery as a class of objects and as a workplace. It is important to preserve the skill and lore of the craftsperson who changes a basic raw material from its amorphous state to a useful entity. It is important to preserve the option of a fabricating process in which one individual is responsible for both design and execution by means of the workmanship of risk. It is important to preserve the goal of the pursuit of artistic quality in an entrepreneurial setting. All these situations grow rarer and rarer, yet they are the laboratory in which progress and invention are born.

This is similar to the plea for the preservation of genetic diversity in the animal and plant kingdoms. Survival, especially in times of crisis and change, depends upon the flexibility of response possible only when there are many options. We cannot know the shape of the future. Indeed, we can hardly perceive the shape of the time in which we live. We can only dedicate ourselves to those activities we find meaningful and believe would be relevant in the best of all possible worlds. Perhaps as society catches up and matures into the age of information, the manufacturing of many domestic items will once again become the meeting place of individuality, quality, and necessity. The inequities of the current times are troubling and confusing for the potter but do not obviate the value of the craft.

A training experience in a specific tradition such as I had can hardly be found today. It was unique not only in its ties to utilitarianism and sound form as modeled by the past but also in the conviction imported from Zen Buddhism that the pursuit of excellence in the crafts was an activity of the highest spiritual order. Contemporary students who want to make utilitarian pots are participating in the overarching tradition of the wheel and its morphological possibilities, but they will have to deliberately choose their pottery styles and attitudes and grow into them. Once the commitment is made and the hard work embraced, the life of a potter is entirely sustaining.

Notes

Truth to Process

1. Bernard Leach, *A Potter's Book* (London: Faber and Faber, 1940), 20–21.

Wondrous

1. David Pye, *The Nature and Art of Workmanship* (Bethel, Conn.: Cambium Press, 1995), 20, 45.
2. Milan Kundera, *The Book of Laughter and Forgetting* (New York: Harper Perennial, 1996), 225–226.
3. Cyril Stanley Smith, *A Search for Structure: Selected Essays on Science, Art, and History* (Cambridge, Mass.: MIT Press, 1981), 388.

The Space Within

1. Jack Troy, "Jugology: The Neurological Origins of Wheel-Thrown Pottery," *American Ceramics* 1, no. 2 (spring 1982): 28–31.

Cylinders as Pots

1. Philip Rawson, *Ceramics: An Appreciation* (London: Oxford University Press, 1971), 82.
2. William Daley, "The Geometry of Residence," *NCECA Journal* 4 (1983): 23.
3. Flannery O'Connor, *Mystery and Manners* (New York: Farrar, Straus and Giroux, 1969), 92.

Pitchers

1. Frank Hamer, *The Potter's Dictionary of Materials and Techniques* (London: Pitman Publishing, 1975), 153.

Learning to See

1. Rawson, *Ceramics*, 104.
2. Janet Koplos, "Gail Kendall," *American Ceramics* 2, no. 1 (winter 1983): 59.
3. Arthur Danto, "Artifact and Art," in *Art/artifact*, ed. Susan M. Vogel, 2nd ed. (New York: Prestel, Verlas and Center for African Art, 1989), 23.
4. Gregory Bateson, *Mind and Nature* (New York: Bantam Books, 1980), 13–14.
5. Ibid., 13, 9.
6. György Doczi, *The Power of Limits* (Boulder, Colo: Shambhala Publications, 1981), 133.
7. Ibid., 2, 13.
8. Ibid., 52.

Style and Voice

1. Pye, *The Nature and Art*, 34–37.

Utility and Tradition

1. Rose Krebs, "A Dornburg Apprentice," in *Studio Potter* 10, no. 1 (December 1981): 63.
2. Doczi, *The Power*.

Place

1. Smith, *A Search*, 326.
2. Bateson, *Mind and Nature*, 197.
3. Pye, *The Nature and Art*, 83–84.
4. Eileen Boris, *Art and Labor: Ruskin, Morris, and the Craftsman Ideal in America* (Philadelphia: Temple University Press, 1986), 191–193.
5. Chris Staley, "Personal Reflections," *Ceramic Monthly* 35, no. 2 (December 1987): 40.